THE
ПO BLÅCK
PROJECT

THE LIFE CHANGING WAY TO CREATE AN EFFORTLES MIX AND MATCH WARDROBE

NUMBA PINKERTON

LEGAL DISCLAIMER

The information in this book is provided and sold with the knowledge that the publisher and author make no representations or warranties with respect to the accuracy or completeness of the contents of this work and specifically disclaim all warranties, including without limitation warranties for fitness for a particular purpose. This book has not been created to be specific to any individual's situation or needs. The advice and strategies contained in this book may not be suitable for every situation. This book does not contain all information available on the subject. The images in this book are for illustrative purposes only.

Every effort has been made to make this book as accurate as possible. However, there may be typographical and or content errors. Therefore, this book should serve only as a general guide and not as the ultimate source of subject information. This book contains information that might be dated and is intended only to educate and entertain. Furthermore, readers should be aware that internet websites listed in this work may have changed or disappeared between when the work was written and when it is read. The fact that an organisation or website is referred to in this work as a citation and/or a potential source of further information does not mean that the author or publisher endorses the information, the organisation or website it may provide or recommendations it may make.

The author and publisher shall have no liability or responsibility to any person or entity regarding any loss or damage incurred, or alleged to have incurred, directly or indirectly, by the information contained in this book. You hereby agree to be bound by this disclaimer.

DEDICATION

This book is dedicated to all my clients who inspired this topic and have made my job the most exciting job I could ever have dreamed of.

ACKNOWLEDGEMENTS

To my son, *Spencer* for giving me the courage to start and complete this book.

To *Kevin* and *Mum* for believing in me.

To my *Family* and *Friends* for their support and encouragement every step of the way.

To all the *Brands* and *Retailers* that have inspired my style choices and 'The No Black Project'.

CONTENTS

INTRODUCTION

THE NO BLACK PROJECT

Acountless number of recent surveys have revealed that most women only wear 20% of the clothes in their wardrobe, yet spend a considerable amount of time and money buying more and more clothing and accessories. The end result is that most women find themselves in a style rut. You are in a style rut if: You feel like you have nothing to wear despite having a full wardrobe; you waste lots of time and energy on deciding what to wear; you find it difficult to figure out what goes with what; or you keep falling back into wearing the same outfit. Luckily, help is at hand!

As a professional Personal Stylist, I have seen first-hand how much time and effort women go through in trying to create a wardrobe that works efficiently for them. My clients are not celebrities or extremely wealthy people; they are normal, real people just like you and me, with real lifestyles and real budgets! I have spent the last few years helping many clients find fun in fashion, develop their personal style and create wardrobes that are both flattering and in line with their lifestyles. I want my clients to open their wardrobes and feel joyful at having countless flattering options for any occasion. I want my clients to feel great in what they are wearing, and more importantly, I want my clients to look effortlessly stylish, yet be able to free up plenty of time to focus on the things that truly matter to them in life.

Most women who have come to me in the past for consultations have claimed that their wardrobe is full of black. They feel like they are stuck in a style rut and want some ideas to add more style variety and colour to their wardrobes. If this sounds familiar, then this book is for you. Let me make it perfectly clear that there is nothing wrong with wearing black; in fact, I personally own a few black pieces in my wardrobe. The aim of this book is not to stop you from buying or wearing black. It is simply to open your eyes to many other alternative colours (and shades) that you can wear and the idea that reducing the amount of black in your wardrobe will in fact dramatically make for a better, more versatile wardrobe.

Can you imagine not wearing black? The idea of not wearing much black scares the life out of many women. For those of you with lots of black in your wardrobes, I would like to question whether your attachment to wearing black is simply a fashion convenience, an easy way out of expressing yourself and your creativity, or perhaps an addictive habit you gradually developed over time. Perhaps the truth is in all three statements. If this is you, my hope is that this book fundamentally saves you from your attachment to black or at the very least, provides you with some useful information and inspiration to help you discover the many alternative colours and shades to black that will help you create a versatile mix and match wardrobe that you absolutely love!

This book is not about 'What styles suit your body shape' or 'What specific colours suit you'. There are plenty of books on that. This is a book that will teach you the skills to create a great mix and match wardrobe and help you look effortlessly stylish for any occasion. This book is not meant to be an all-round 'Bible' of 'must have items'. It is impossible to create a 'one-size-fits-all' book for all the different body shapes, colourings, lifestyles and possible occasions. Each of us is unique and beautiful in our own way. Regardless of your colouring, body shape, size or lifestyle; use this book as a guide to help you create a versatile wardrobe with only a few pieces that will go a long way. The book is intentionally written in plain, simple, English to make understanding style and creating a capsule wardrobe easy.

By following the guidelines in this book, you will be simplifying your wardrobe and your life significantly: You will save lots of time and money on the wrong purchases, have fewer clothes in your wardrobe, spend very little time getting dressed in the morning and look fabulous for any occasion with little effort. Your wardrobe will coordinate a lot better and your choices will be much more obvious. You will have less clothing, yet have an outfit for every occasion. You will not have to rely on black every time you get dressed.

So, embrace and enjoy creating your ultimate stylish and versatile wardrobe!

CHAPTER 1

CHAPTER 1

- IT ALL BEGINS WITH YOU -

"To lose confidence in one's body
is to lose confidence in oneself."

— Simone de Beauvoir

YOU AND YOUR BODY

H ave you noticed how someone you know always seems to pull off different styles and colours? They seem to always look relaxed, well-put together and confident in what they are wearing. "How do they do it?" you wonder…the answer is simple. They love themselves unconditionally- This empowers them and gives them confidence.

Most of us know that loving ourselves unconditionally is integral to our own personal happiness and spiritual growth. Yet, we can't help but feel apathy towards our bodies sometimes. In fact, I have been approached by many beautiful clients who have had many negative things to say about their bodies. They simply do not feel that their bodies are good enough. They look at their bodies with hate or disgust, wish they were slimmer or taller, wish their bust was bigger or smaller and wish their tummy was flatter… the list goes on. Most women tend to focus on parts of their bodies that they don't love and completely ignore the parts of their bodies that they do love.

So, why is it so hard for us to love ourselves and accept the appearance of our bodies? I strongly believe that social conditioning and the habit of comparing ourselves to others are the biggest causes of our insecurities. We are easily led to believe that we need to look a certain way or have the latest fashion trend in order to be happy. We convince ourselves that we will only feel happy within ourselves when we 'buy that expensive dress' or 'lose that extra two stone'. This makes us feel insecure and worthless which in turn causes us to buy more and more products in the hope that they make us feel better about ourselves.

YOU ARE SO MUCH MORE THAN JUST YOUR BODY

What we essentially forget is that as human beings, we are not just our body; we are also mind and spirit which is our entire 'selfhood'. Most of us women feel that our physical identity and our selfhood are split. We have a definite divide between 'who we are' and 'what we look like'. Instead of looking at our whole selves - we see individual components, to be judged accordingly.

There is no such thing as ideal or perfect. The truth is; each one of us is unique and beautiful in our own right. It is time to stop this body shaming and start to embrace your own unique qualities. It is time to focus on your strengths rather than your weaknesses. It is time to stop judging and start living with full appreciation and acceptance of your body, regardless of what shape or size you are. It is time to start loving yourself fully. You are so much more than just your body!

APPRECIATION AND ACCEPTANCE

Loving yourself starts with appreciation and acceptance. Acceptance means being aware of your body, your strengths and weaknesses yet fully accepting all of you. Everybody's body is different. Unique. Beautiful. There is no such thing as perfection. The more you appreciate what the body does for you, from walking you everywhere to digesting your food to fighting against illnesses; the more you appreciate what you have instead of what you don't have, you will begin to look at your body in a different light.

Having a different body from someone else doesn't make

yours any less attractive. You were created as a beautiful being with all your features carefully planted where they should be, in perfect harmony with your body; that's what makes you unique and beautiful. You have a body for a reason; and this reason is not to win admiration from others. It's not to make other people feel bad about themselves, or to make you feel bad about yourself. Your body serves a purpose. It is built to house who you are.

The more you focus on looking after your body through good nutrition and exercise (rather than 'trying to lose weight'), the more your body will serve you and make you feel good about yourself.

RESPECT OTHERS

Some of us women have a tendency to be our own greatest critic. However, we don't just do this to ourselves; we do this to other women too: "Did you see the size of her arms? She really should not be wearing that dress!" "She really should not be wearing those skinny jeans- She is too fat for them!" We need to stop judging and start accepting. How can we imagine that we'll be able to respect our bodies unless we also respect others? It's time for us to collectively decide to respect every shape and size and honour every physique. If you're pointing out flaws in others, then you're simply projecting your own inner fears.

When you begin to see other women as the beautiful people they are, you will have a much easier time loving who you are. When you appreciate other people's personal style, you will begin to appreciate your own. Stop looking for faults, inadequacies, imperfections and start seeing and appreciating ourselves, and others, as a whole. A body, mind and spirit working together to create the wonderful, unique woman you are.

DRESS FOR THE BODY YOU HAVE NOW

I have met many women who claim they are waiting to lose weight before doing anything about their style, wardrobe or appearance. It always saddens me to hear this. What if it takes you 10 years to reach your ideal weight? What if you die next week? Will you sacrifice looking your best and feeling joyful today for an unknown future? You deserve to

THE NO BLACK PROJECT

look your best TODAY regardless of your shape, size or age; not tomorrow, not next month, not in a year's time or 5 years' time- TODAY.

You deserve to have a wardrobe that ties in with your current body, your personality and lifestyle. If you still have clothing in your wardrobe that you wore when you were a smaller size that you are hoping to fit into again, thinking maybe, just maybe you will be able to wear it again someday, then it is time to ditch them. They will make you feel worse about yourself and your body. Dress for the body you have now, not the body you had then or the body you think you will have in the future.

DEVELOP YOUR CONFIDENCE

I have come across clients who would love something they see in a shop but claim that it would look better on someone else even when I know it will look amazing on them! This comes from a lack of confidence. In order to develop confidence, you must first change your behaviours, thoughts and perceptions of yourself. If you perceive yourself as being unattractive, awkward and not stylish, then this is what you will believe, how you will see yourself and how you will act. You will become this person.

In my experience, one of the best ways to become confident is to build on it over time through action and competence. For every action you take, you will surprise yourself at just how much you can do. You can always do more than you think you can. Style Confidence is all about having an educated style and being in control of how you present yourself, ensuring that what you wear reflects how you feel, your personality and unique strengths. When your style is at its best, your time and energy can be directed to other important areas of your life. Like everything else, style confidence comes from knowledge and skill. My hope is that this book helps to enhance your style confidence by building on your knowledge and skills.

CHAPTER 2

CHAPTER 2

- THE SECRETS TO WARDROBE SUCCESS -

"Embracing your personal style means expressing yourself or your personality through what you wear instead of wearing what is dictated by fashion trends."

— Numba Pinkerton

D o you love every single piece in your wardrobe? Most of us will struggle to answer a strong yes to this question. From past experience, quantity is never an issue for most women's wardrobes. Most of us have overflowing wardrobes, yet only wear a small percentage of what we own. We dread opening our wardrobes and getting dressed in the morning. We spend fortunes on clothing and accessories; yet, this does not translate into wearing stylish outfits that we feel good in. The weird thing is that the more we have in our wardrobes, often the less we have to wear.

What if you could take more control over your wardrobe and your style? What if you could go to your wardrobe tomorrow morning, grab the first thing you see, put it on and look fabulous? What if you could do it the next day…and the next? How about every day for the rest of your life? Sounds impossible? Wrong! I did it, and so have many other women all over the world. There are some secrets to style and wardrobe success. With some willpower and patience, you too can have a successful mix and match wardrobe.

BE YOUR OWN EDUCATED STYLIST

Being your own educated stylist means understanding your personal values and personality, knowing your body, colouring and personal style. It means having knowledge about colour and style and being able to apply it to your wardrobe without compromising your personality, values or lifestyle. Becoming your own educated stylist will help you make better decisions about what you buy, how you manage your wardrobe and how you pick and create outfits for different occasions. Having knowledge about how to mix and match clothing and accessories will fundamentally enhance your style and image. Reading a style book, taking a short course or hiring a personal stylist can help you become your own educated stylist and make the most of your style and wardrobe.

UNDERSTAND YOUR PERSONAL STYLE

One of the secrets to great style is to really understand your personality and style preferences. Each woman has a personal style of some form. You will tend to prefer certain types of garments and outfits over others which will reflect your nature, lifestyle or personality. Embracing your personal style means expressing yourself or your personality through what you wear instead of wearing what is dictated by fashion trends. I personally do not believe in 'labelling' your personal style. Your personal style should be based on what you love and what resonates with you the most! This could change over time or fluctuate based on how you feel that day or the occasion you are dressing for.

'Personal style' is about being true to yourself. It's about being willing to use blogs, books, courses and expert advice as guidance and then being willing to add your own stamp on it. In order to work in line with your personal style, you must always LOVE what you buy and how it looks on you. Being comfortable in what you wear and being true to your style personality will make you feel more confident and help you create a wardrobe that's in keeping with your personal style and lifestyle.

EVALUATE YOUR LIFESTYLE

Many of my clients come to me when they feel stuck in a rut and are not sure what needs to be done to get them out of it. They have plenty of clothes in the wardrobe but still struggle to get dressed in the morning. This is partly caused by failing to take into consideration your lifestyle when building your wardrobe and shopping for clothing and accessories. In a perfect world, your wardrobe should be proportional to your lifestyle. Think about what activities you do during a normal week and how much time you spend on each activity then tailor your wardrobe to suit your lifestyle. For example, if you spend the majority of your time working, the majority of clothing and accessories in your wardrobe should be pieces that that you can wear to work and effectively mix and match to create a range of outfits specifically for work.

KEEP YOUR WARDROBE CLUTTER FREE

Your wardrobe is not just a place where your clothing is hung and stored. It is a place where you are creating yourself and your life. Hanging on to clothing and accessories, that you don't fit into, clothing that you have not worn for many years, or clothing you do not love creates clutter and detracts from some of your most exciting, wearable and functional pieces in your wardrobe. Clutter will make you feel out of control, helpless and can sometimes cause stress which easily transfers into other areas of your life. De-cluttering will remind you of what you do have in your wardrobe, create more space for clothing that you will wear and help you plan better for your shopping trips. Keeping your wardrobe clutter-free gives you control of your wardrobe and consequently, your life.

PLAN YOUR SHOPPING TRIPS

Planning your shopping trip will save you lots of time and money on impulse buys. There is no right or wrong answer when it comes to how often you should shop. I tend to plan two big shopping trips a year, usually when the sales are on in the UK (after winter and after summer) and prioritising buying my essentials- items of clothing I wear the most. This will normally include jeans, blazers and ankle boots). I then sparingly buy a few other items during the year. Having said that, every woman is different, therefore, my advice is to come up with a plan that works for you.

FIND A GOOD TAILOR

Having a good local tailor can save you huge amounts of money and problems when it comes to the fit of clothing. From my experience shopping for clients in the past, one size does not fit all. Women come in many different shapes and proportions; which means some of us will naturally struggle to get the right fit, especially when it comes to long sleeved tops, skirts and trousers. Struggling to find the right length to suit you is very common. Many people will get rid of perfectly good clothing simply because it does not fit properly! What most women forget is that it costs very little to get clothing altered by a professional tailor. When shopping, concentrate on getting the right fit on your shoulders or hips and leave the rest to your local tailor.

CHAPTER 3

CHAPTER 3

- A SIMPLE GUIDE TO PICKING COLOURS -

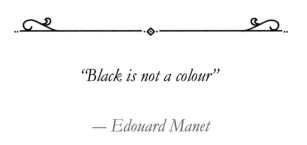

"Black is not a colour"

— Edouard Manet

Having worked with colour for so many years, I cannot stress enough how important colour is in style and fashion. Colour is the ultimate key to looking your best; it is the backbone of style. In order to mix and match your clothing, shoes and accessories effectively, a thorough understanding of colour is required. Most people think of colour as a hue (pure colours) such as red, blue, yellow, green, etc. However, there are scientifically many variations of these colours based on tint (pure colour +white), tone (Hue +grey) and shade (hue + black). For the purpose of this book, I am referring to shades as a collective term to describe hues, tints, tones and shades of each colour.

This chapter is not about in-depth 'colour analysis' or 'what specific colours suit you'; there are many books on that. Although I will provide some guidance on what shades might look better on you, this chapter is mainly about making the concept of colour and colour matching easy to understand and apply to your wardrobe. With this knowledge, you can easily coordinate your wardrobe, and therefore extend the use of all clothes and accessories.

IMPORTANCE OF COLOUR

Colour is the first thing we notice (consciously or sub-consciously) when shopping, picking an outfit from our wardrobes or interacting with other people. The fact is; you have the freedom to wear any colour you want. However, not all colours and shades will look amazing on you. History tells us that there is a definite relationship between choice of colour, personal appearance and personality. It is always a good idea to be guided by shades which suit your natural colouring - that is; your skin tone, eye colour and hair colour. Whether you are aware of it or not, the shades you wear reflect onto your face and have a huge impact on your appearance. The right shades can make your skin tone appear more even; reducing the appearance of dark circles and skin imperfections such as redness, wrinkles, etc. The right shades can also make you look brighter, healthier and alert. On the other hand, wearing shades that do not complement your natural colouring can make you look tired, dull, drained and even ill. So why spend money on something that does not enhance your natural colouring or makes you look worse off than you actually are?

A SHADE FOR EVERYONE

Wearing your best range of shades can have a huge impact on your wardrobe and your confidence. I personally believe that there is a shade for everyone in most colours. I therefore prefer to shift the focus from 'colours' to 'shades'. For example, I know that shades of pink such as Rose pink or Fuchsia pink will complement my colouring better than Coral Pink or Salmon Pink. Look in your wardrobe and see how many different colours you own. Do you have a range of colours and shades, or does your wardrobe look quite monochrome? You may find that your wardrobe is lacking colour, or that your wardrobe is extremely colourful. Either way, the problem most women face is knowing how to mix and match these colours or shades. Having an idea of what range of shades look better on you will help you make better decisions about choosing different colours when shopping or putting outfits together. You will buy fewer clothes, but have a suitable outfit for all occasions.

YOUR GO TO COLOUR PALETTES

From past experience, there are two main colour palettes (groups) containing different shades that will make the biggest difference when mixing and matching clothing and accessories. I will refer to them as the 'Sunlight Palette' and the 'Moonlight Palette.' There is a third palette I call the 'Universal Palette' which consists of a combination of 'Sunlight' and 'Moonlight' Shades and will tend to look good on most people. All palettes contain a mix of light/dark shades as well as bright/muted shades. The important thing to remember is not to get too strict over these specifics.

SUNLIGHT SHADES

Ivory | Cream | Stone Grey | Taupe | Beige | Carmel | Tan | Dark Brown | Orange

Burnt Orange | Mustard | Warm Yellow | Light Peach | Deep Peach | Salmon | Coral | Mango | Tomato Red

Bittersweet Red | Rust | Deep Khaki | Khaki | Lime Green | Pastel Yellow Green | Forest Green | Olive | Teal

Turquoise | Emerald Turquoise | Navy | Periwinkle | Hyacinth Blue | Aqua | Purple | Warm Violet | Gold

Sunlight shades are warm in nature. These are shades that have a yellow undertone to them. When you look at sunlight colours, they look 'yellowy' and 'feel' quite 'warm'.

*Sunlight Shades remind you of the sun.

MOONLIGHT SHADES

| Soft White | Stone Grey | Taupe | Light Grey | Medium Grey | Charcoal | Pewter | Navy | Black |

| Deep Brown | Silver | Soft Pink | Medium Pink | Powder Pink | Deep Pink | Magenta | Soft Fuchsia | Blue Red |

| Cranberry | Burgundy | True Red | Powder Blue | Sky Blue | True Blue | Cobalt Blue | Bright Periwinkle | Purple |

| Lavender | Medium Aqua | Emerald Turquoise | Teal | Light Teal | Mint Green | Emerald Green | True Green | Icy Yellow |

Moonlight shades are shades that have a blue undertone to them. When you look at cool colours, they look 'bluey' and 'feel' quite 'cold.'

*Moonlight shades do not remind you of the sun. They remind you of ice, cold, or the moon itself.

The best way to tell the difference between sunlight shades and moonlight shades is to look out for the 'yellowness' or 'warmth'. If the shade is yellowy and reminds you of the sun, then the shade will be a sunlight shade. If, on the other hand, the shade does not look 'yellowy' or does not remind you of the sun, then the shade is a moonlight shade.

UNIVERSAL SHADES

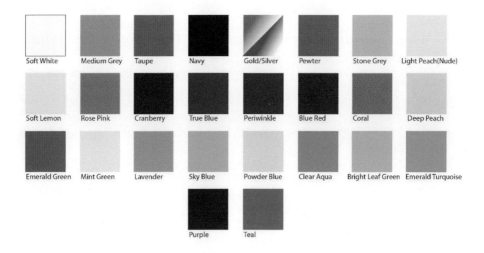

Soft White · Medium Grey · Taupe · Navy · Gold/Silver · Pewter · Stone Grey · Light Peach(Nude)

Soft Lemon · Rose Pink · Cranberry · True Blue · Periwinkle · Blue Red · Coral · Deep Peach

Emerald Green · Mint Green · Lavender · Sky Blue · Powder Blue · Clear Aqua · Bright Leaf Green · Emerald Turquoise

Purple · Teal

Universal shades are shades that I have put together from the Sunlight and Moonlight palette that will tend to look good on most people, hence the term 'Universal'. The Universal palette contains both **Sunlight** and **Moonlight shades**.

NEUTRAL COLOURS

Neutral colours are the foundation of a good, functional wardrobe. When building a wardrobe, it is a good idea to build your wardrobe based on neutral classics and style staples. These items are referred to as your 'base' and include Items that can easily be dressed up or dressed down such as trousers, jackets, skirts and dresses.

Each colour palette will contain some neutral colours. The Sunlight palette will contain what I refer to as 'Sunlight Neutrals' and the Moonlight palette will contain what I refer to as 'Moonlight Neutrals'. Neutral colours will match any colour in their palette. Therefore, Sunlight Neutrals will match any colour in the Sunlight palette and Moonlight Neutrals will match any colour in the Moonlight palette. The Universal Palette will contain both Sunlight and Moonlight Neutrals.

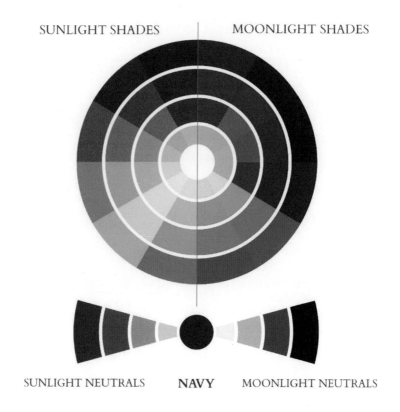

SUNLIGHT SHADES | MOONLIGHT SHADES

SUNLIGHT NEUTRALS   **NAVY**   MOONLIGHT NEUTRALS

'Sunlight Neutrals' include: Dark brown, Light Brown, Beige and Cream White

'Moonlight Neutrals' include: Black, Charcoal grey, Medium grey, Light Grey and Pure White.

'Universal Neutrals' Include: 'Moonlight Neutrals'- Soft White, Medium Grey, Taupe, Navy, Silver and 'Sunlight Neutrals'- Gold, Pewter, Stone grey and Nude/ Light Peach.

NAVY IS THE NEW BLACK

Although navy is a Moonlight shade, I refer to it as the **'ultimate universal shade'** because it looks great on everybody and will work well with **any colour** to create a harmony in an outfit. Therefore, any colour in the Sunlight, Moonlight or Universal Palette will work well with navy. Contrary to popular belief; Black, on the other hand, does not work well (blend harmoniously) with just any colour! Black is a Moonlight Neutral and only tends to work well with colours from the Moonlight Palette.

GUIDE TO PICKING THE BEST PALETTE FOR YOU

There are no set rules here about which palette you should choose. However, here are some basic guidelines for choosing a palette to suit you:

Method 1: Using the following guidelines to discover what palette will look better on you.

<u>**Sunlight palette:**</u>

You will look better in SUNLIGHT shades if most of the statements below apply to you:

- Your skin has yellow undertones (i.e. Your skin looks 'yellowy' rather than 'pinky' or 'rosy')
- You tan easily when exposed to lots of sun or have lots of freckles
- Your hair has golden, yellow, red or orange tones to it. Your hair colour could range from dark golden brown to light golden blond.
- You look better in gold jewellery close to your face than you do in silver jewellery (Not which you *like*

more, but which actually makes you look more radiant).

- Your skin looks better in ivory or cream white rather than pure white.

Moonlight Palette

You will look better in MOONLIGHT shades if most of the statements below apply to you:

- Your skin has pink or rose undertones (i.e. You skin looks 'pinky' or 'rosy' rather than 'yellowy')
- You tend to burn first before you tan when exposed to lots of sun.
- Your hair has ash, blue, silver and tones to it. Your hair colour can range from dark brown/black to blond.
- You look better in silver jewellery close to your face than you do in gold jewellery (Not which you *like* more, but which actually makes you look more radiant).
- Your skin looks better in pure white rather than ivory or cream.

Method 2: Choose the Palette you Love

The simplest way to make a decision about which palette to choose either for building a full wardrobe, shopping or simply creating an outfit is by picking the palette you intuitively love the most. Which one are you drawn to? Which one makes you feel excited? Which one reflects your personality? Go for it!

CHANGING YOUR HAIR COLOUR COULD AFFECT YOUR COLOURING

If you find that the shades you love don't look particularly look great on you, your current hair colour may not be in line with your true colouring or the colours you love. The good news is; this can easily be fixed!

Changing your hair colour will have a huge effect on your overall appearance which will impact on which shades look better on you. If you prefer a specific palette you could change your hair colour to suit the shades in that palette. For example, my personal go-to palette is the Moonlight palette because it matches my complexion and hair colour. If I changed my hair colour to a golden brown, or golden blonde (which I have done in the past), my Moonlight shades would no longer look as good on me as if I had kept the black hair or changed it to a Moonlight hair shade such as light ash brown.

Here is some guidance on how to identify your current hair shade:

Sunlight Hair: Sunlight hair has golden, yellow, red or orange tones to it. Your hair colour could range from dark golden brown to light golden blonde.

Moonlight Hair: Moonlight hair has ash, blue or silver tones to it. Your hair colour can range from dark brown/black to light ash-blonde.

Here is some guidance on hair shades for each palette:

Sunlight hair shades: Auburn, Dark golden brown, Medium golden brown, Light golden brown, Medium golden blond, Light golden blonde and Strawberry blonde.

Moonlight hair shades: Jet black, Deep Brown, Burgundy, Medium ash brown, Light ash brown, Burgundy, Medium ash blonde, Light ash blonde and Platinum blonde.

Universal hair shades: Chocolate Brown, Mahogany, Sandy blonde and Beige blonde.

Next time you get your hair coloured or visit your

hairdresser, buy a suitable shade or ask your hair dresser to use a shade in line with your chosen palette.

Method 3: Choose a Palette according to how you feel that day

Although I would recommend choosing only one palette to work with for effortless mixing and matching, you may find that you have a combination of both Sunlight and Moonlight shades in your wardrobe. If this is the case, simply pick a colour you want to wear on that day, identify if the colour/shade is in the sunlight or moonlight palette, then work with other colours/shades in that palette. For example, if I feel like wearing a red top one day and I have identified it as being a shade of red in the Sunlight palette; I can work with other colours in the Sunlight palette to create a suitable outfit.

HOW TO DIFFERENTIATE SUNLIGHT SHADES FROM MOONLIGHT SHADES

Although referring to your chosen colour palette will help you with the mixing and matching process, going a step further in learning how to correctly identify Sunlight or Moonlight shades in clothing and accessories will enable you to save lots of time, energy and money when putting an outfit together or shopping. It also means you don't have to rely too heavily on constantly referring to your palettes. However, do not worry if you do not understand this section. You will always have your colour palettes to fall back on.

Recognising the difference between Sunlight and Moonlight shades is easy! All you have to do is train your eye into being able to tell the difference between the two.

Sunlight colours will **remind you of the sun.** When you look at sunlight colours, they look 'yellowy' and 'feel' quite 'warm'.

Moonlight colours will **remind you of cold, ice or the**

moon. When you look at cool colours, they look 'bluey' and 'feel' quite 'icy' or 'cold.'

** When training yourself to recognise the difference between sunlight and moonlight shades, the key is to avoid associating these shades with the colours you like or how bright, muted, dark or light a colour is at this point. The reality is; you can get a 'bright' Sunlight shade and a 'bright' Moonlight shade. The key is to look beyond the lightness/darkness or brightness of a colour and focus on its overall undertone.

EXAMPLE: THE DIFFERENCE BETWEEN SUNLIGHT AND
MOONLIGHT SHADES

The figure below shows the difference between Sunlight
Shades and Moonlight Shades:

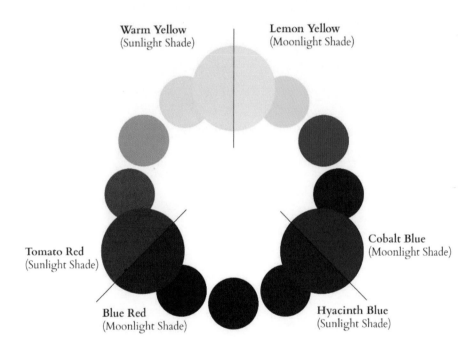

If you are not sure, simply ask yourself this powerful question:

"Does this colour/shade remind me of the sun?" Is it yellowy?

If the answer is **YES,** then the shade is a **Sunlight shade**

If the answer is **NO,** then the shade is a **Moonlight shade**

Practice by analysing different colours in your wardrobe and you will soon get the hang of it. When you do, mixing and matching becomes so much easier!

IDENTIFYING SUNLIGHT SHADES AND MOONLIGHT SHADES WITH PATTERNS

The above concept also applies for patterns. The only difference is, you would need to identify what the **overall colouring** of a garment is rather than looking at smaller, individual colours separately. This should take seconds. Do not over-analyse!

Again, ask yourself the question: **Does this garment remind me of the sun overall?**

Yes = Sunlight shade

No = Moonlight shade

Sometimes, the colouring of a particular garment is likely to be exactly on the line between the two (Sunlight and Moonlight) due to the combination of colours- If this is the case, then the pattern is **'Universal'** and will look ok on anyone. When in doubt, simply try it on and determine whether it looks good on you or not.

EXAMPLES OF SUNLIGHT, MOONLIGHT AND UNIVERSAL
PATTERNS

SUNLIGHT
PATTERN

MOONLIGHT
PATTERN

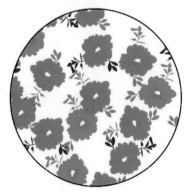

UNIVERSAL
PATTERN

REMEMBER:

From past experience, not everyone can tell the difference between Sunlight and Moonlight shades. If you are one of these people, please don't despair. Whilst being able to recognise Sunlight shades and Moonlight shades when you see them is beneficial, you can still learn to mix and match effectively simply by referring to your chosen colour palette to keep you right.

If you are not sure whether a pattern falls under 'Sunlight' or 'Moonlight', its probably because the colour is between the two, which will look good on either a Sunlight or Moonlight person.

Blue jeans are 'Universal' because they are shades of Navy which works with any colour. Black and medium or dark Grey jeans will only work with other moonlight colours.

CHAPTER 4

CHAPTER 4

- THE LIFE CHANGING WAY TO MIX AND MATCH -

"I don't really have a secret. I just try to wear matching colours"

— *-Ben Striller*

From my experience working with many clients, I have come to realise that most women's wardrobe issues stem from having too many clothes and accessories; yet not knowing how to put outfits together. As discussed in the previous chapter, colour is the most important factor to consider when mixing and matching. By simply learning how different shades work together, you will be empowered to create an amazing range of outfits effortlessly. In this chapter, you will discover the easiest ways to create different outfit combinations simply by understanding how to mix and match colours and shades. Once you get the hang of it, you will be putting lots of fun, amazing outfits together in no time!

HOW TO MIX AND MATCH COLOURS

Learning to mix and match colour will dramatically improve how you put outfits together and make more use of your clothing and accessories. Although using a colour wheel can be effective in mixing and matching, past experience has taught me that most of us will not have the time or patience to dig out a colour wheel early in the morning when we need to get dressed fast!

There is a simpler way to mix and match clothing and accessories:

WEAR SUNLIGHT SHADES WITH OTHER SUNLIGHT SHADES

OR

WEAR MOONLIGHT SHADES WITH OTHER MOONLIGHT SHADES

Sounds too simple? That's because it is!

Using this method, you do not have to think about matching actual colours. The focus is simply on using the right shades from each palette. If you can remember what a Sunlight shade should look like (yellow undertones and reminds you of the sun) and what a Moonlight shade should like (blue undertones and does not remind you of the sun), you can easily throw clothes on as long as they belong to your chosen palette.

The fact is, whether your item of clothing or accessory is patterned or not, as long as you match what you identify as a Sunlight shade with another Sunlight shade or a Moonlight shade with another moonlight shade, they will definitely match.

EXAMPLES

1. WEAR SUNLIGHT SHADES WITH OTHER SUNLIGHT SHADES

| Ivory | Cream | Stone Grey | Taupe | Beige | Carmel | Tan | Dark Brown | Orange |

| Burnt Orange | Mustard | Warm Yellow | Light Peach | Deep Peach | Salmon | Coral | Mango | Tomato Red |

| Bittersweet Red | Rust | Deep Khaki | Khaki | Lime Green | Pastel Yellow Green | Forest Green | Olive | Teal |

| Turquoise | Emerald Turquoise | Navy | Periwinkle | Hyacinth Blue | Aqua | Purple | Warm Violet | Gold |

2. WEAR MOONLIGHT SHADES WITH OTHER MOONLIGHT SHADES

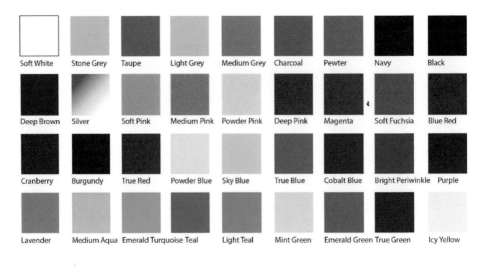

| Soft White | Stone Grey | Taupe | Light Grey | Medium Grey | Charcoal | Pewter | Navy | Black |

| Deep Brown | Silver | Soft Pink | Medium Pink | Powder Pink | Deep Pink | Magenta | Soft Fuchsia | Blue Red |

| Cranberry | Burgundy | True Red | Powder Blue | Sky Blue | True Blue | Cobalt Blue | Bright Periwinkle | Purple |

| Lavender | Medium Aqua | Emerald Turquoise | Teal | Light Teal | Mint Green | Emerald Green | True Green | Icy Yellow |

If you fill your wardrobe with mostly clothing and accessories from only one of the palettes (Sunlight or Moonlight), getting dressed and putting an outfit together will become a lot easier. The quicker you can master the difference between Sunlight shades and Moonlight shades, the better your mixing and matching skills will become.

Don't be too strict with yourself: Incorporating only one shade from the opposite palette in form of bottoms, a bag or shoes can work well because it won't detract from the overall palette/colouring of your outfit, and therefore will not make a huge difference to the overall appearance of the outfit.

If you still do not recognise the difference between the two shades, simply use the palettes provided in this book to get you started. Eventually, you will get to the stage where you can throw clothes on and look amazing for any occasion. You will find yourself not paying too much attention to actual colours yet knowing that most shades in your wardrobe combine well together.

3. WEAR BLUES WITH ORANGE, TAN OR MUSTARD

Naturally, Sunlight shades and Moonlight shades will not work well together, except when specific Shades are matched in form of a colour scheme. I call this mixing and matching method the 'Blue and Orange' method which is derived from one of the colour schemes on the colour wheel.

According to the complementary colour scheme, colours (including their shades) opposite each other on the colour wheel will work well together. Blue and orange as well as blue-violet (which I consider a shade of blue) and yellow-orange (mustard) are exactly opposite on the colour wheel. This implies that you can wear pretty much any shade of blue (such as navy, cobalt blue, sky blue or powder blue) with any shade of orange (such as tan and nude) as well as mustard (yellow-orange).

Therefore, all you have to remember is that:

Blue Works well with Orange, Tan or Mustard

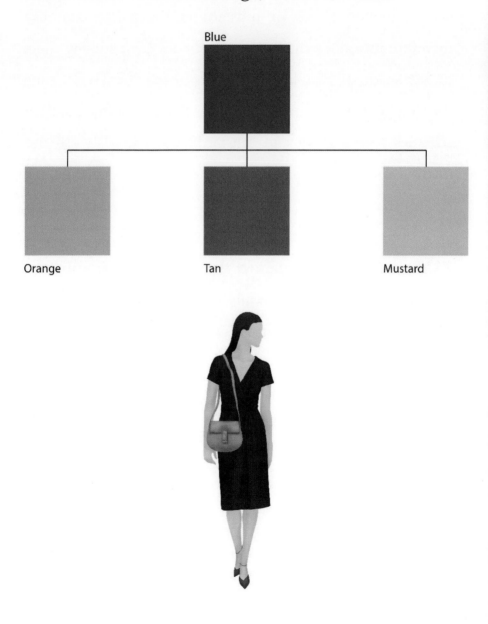

One of the best ways to break up your Moonlight or Sunlight Palette is to specifically use this scheme (The 'Blue and Orange' Scheme). Those using the Moonlight palette do not have orange, tan or mustard in the palette and can therefore introduce these colours/shades by matching them to any shade of blue in the Moonlight palette. Those using the Sunlight palette already have these colours in their schemes (orange, tan and mustard), but can also use this method to match their 'blues' in their palette to orange, tan and mustard.

*Although I have explained the details of this mix and match method, all you really have to remember is that blue works well with orange, tan and mustard.

USING THE UNIVERSAL PALETTE FOR MIXING AND MATCHING

The universal Palette consists of colours and shades that will look good on most people. I have decided to use this palette as a point of reference throughout the rest of the book in order to cater to as many colourings as possible.

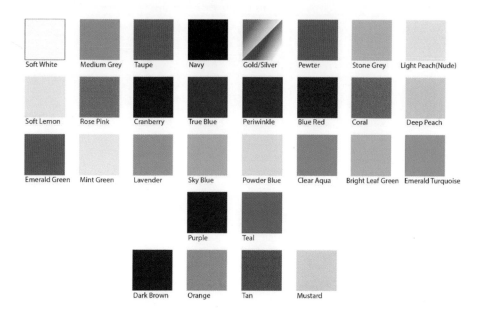

As mentioned in previous chapters, the Universal palette consists of both Sunlight and Moonlight shades. In order to better understand the shades in the Universal palette and use them effectively, I have divided the Universal Palette into five sections as illustrated below which include: Neutrals, Semi Neutrals, Accents, and Limited shades (which include

Orange, Tan and Mustard) so that you can easily incorporate the 'Blue and Orange' mixing and matching method.

UNIVERSAL PALETTE SECTIONS

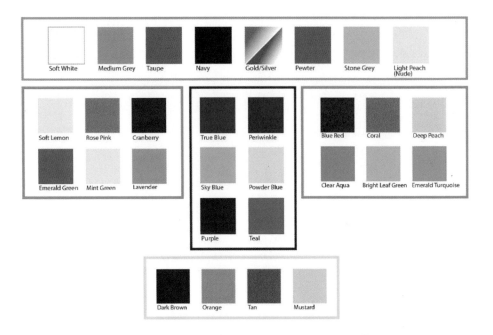

Neutrals (Grey Border): These are Universal Neutrals and will match any shade in the universal palette. Universal neutrals can also be used to 'tone down' your outfit when your outfit colours are 'too bright' or 'too colourful'.

Semi Neutrals (Purple Border): These are shades that will look particularly great with 'limited shades' ('Blues and Orange' mixing and matching scheme) and will also work well with both 'accents' and 'neutrals'.

Accents (Green Border): Accents will add some colour to your outfit and look particularly great in tops and accessories, although they can also be added in form of dresses, skirts or trousers. Use them to 'lift up' your outfit. Accents in the Universal palette consist of 'Moonlight Universal Accents' (Left hand side- Green border) and 'Sunlight Universal Accents' (Right hand side- green border).

Limited Shades (Yellow Border): Limited shades are 'limited' in their use, hence the name. As they are derived from the 'Sunlight' palette, they will ONLY work well with 'Sunlight shades' (including 'Universal Sunlight Accents') or 'Semi neutrals' via the 'Blues and Orange' mixing and matching method. Limited shades will not work well with 'Universal Moonlight Accents'.

HOW TO MIX AND MATCH USING THE UNIVERSAL PALETTE

I have divided the Universal Palette into two main halves: The 'Sunlight Universal Colour Scheme' and the 'Moonlight Universal Colour scheme'. You can choose to use either scheme for mixing and matching purposes. Here are some details of each colour scheme:

1. Colour scheme: Moonlight Universal

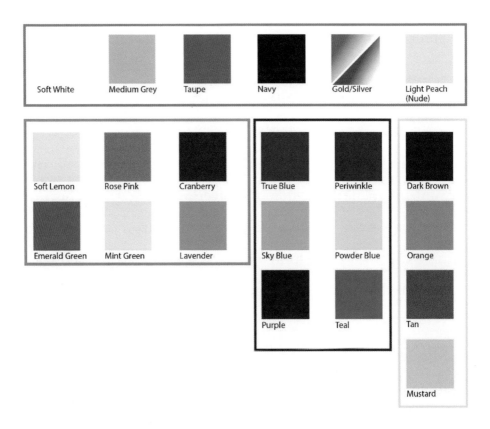

Neutrals (Grey border): Soft white, medium grey, taupe, navy, gold/silver mix, light peach (nude)

Semi Neutrals (Purple border): True blue, periwinkle, sky blue, powder blue, purple, teal

Accents (Green border): soft lemon, rose pink, raspberry, emerald green, mint green, lavender

Limited Shades (Yellow border): Dark brown, orange, tan, mustard

Mixing and matching Method to Use:

- Match Moonlight Universal Shades (Neutrals, Semi neutrals and Accents) with any other Moonlight Universal shades (Neutrals, Semi neutrals and Accents)

  OR

- Use the 'Blue and Orange' mixing and matching method (Match Semi Neutrals with Limited Shades).

2. Colour scheme: Sunlight Universal

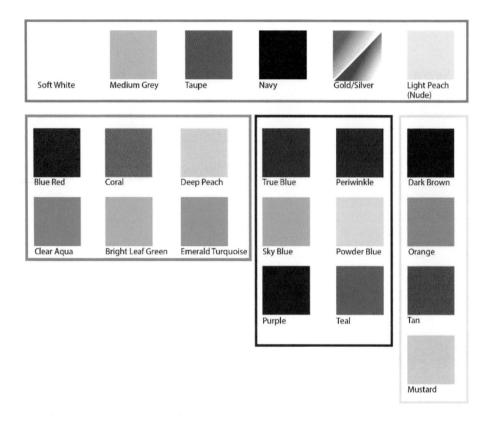

Neutrals (Grey border): Soft white, stone grey, taupe, navy, gold/silver mix, light peach (nude)

Semi Neutrals (Purple border): True blue, periwinkle, sky blue, powder blue, purple, teal

Accents (Green border): blue-red, coral, deep peach, clear aqua, bright leaf green, emerald turquoise

Limited Shades (Yellow border): Dark brown, orange, tan, mustard

Mixing and Matching Method to Use:

- Match Sunlight Universal Shades (Neutrals, Semi neutrals and Accents) With any other Sunlight Universal shades (Neutrals, Semi neutrals and Accents)

OR

- Use the 'Blue and Orange' mixing and matching method (Match Semi Neutrals with Limited Shades).

In the next few chapters, you will be able to see how I have easily used the mixing and matching methods discussed in this chapter to create beautiful outfit combinations for different occasions.

CHAPTER 5

CHAPTER 5

- HOW TO PUT AN OUTFIT TOGETHER -

"To me, accessorising is the most fun part of an outfit. While I don't think you can't rely on accessories to make a dress that isn't working work, I do love jewellery and handbags more than anything."

— - Anna Kendrick

What is so difficult about putting an outfit together, you wonder? Well, the actual act of putting on an outfit is not difficult. The difficult part for most women is ensuring that individual pieces of each outfit are in perfect harmony with each other, that the chosen outfit looks appropriate for the occasion and that it represents you in the best possible light. So how do you go about putting an outfit together?

THINGS TO THINK ABOUT BEFORE PUTTING AN OUTFIT TOGETHER

Before you begin putting an outfit together, you will need to think about several things:

The occasion: First figure out what the occasion is that you are dressing for. This could range from going to work, to meeting a friend for lunch to a night out.

Your outfit in relation to the occasion: Depending on the occasion, your outfit choice might fall under three main categories: Smart casual, Professional work wear and

Evening. You will need to decide which core piece of clothing you would like to wear that day. For example, if the occasion is a relaxed Saturday lunch with friends in town, you may decide to wear jeans, a skirt or a dress.

The image you want to portray: How do you want people to see you? Do you want to stand out or do you want to blend in? These questions will help you figure out what colours/shades to put together.

How you want to feel: The clothing and accessories we choose can impact on how we feel. If we are having a bad day, not feeling good about ourselves or feeling insecure about our bodies, we sometimes tend to automatically choose clothing in dull neutral colours like black because they match how we are feeling. Just as when we are happy, feeling confident within ourselves or the sun is shining, we will tend to go for something lighter or brighter. It is important to remember that you have full control of your feelings through your choice of colours/shades. Remember to dress for how you WANT to feel that day!

Your Chosen Colour Palette: Choosing a colour palette (Sunlight or Moonlight) or colour scheme (Universal palette) to work with will make mixing and matching a lot easier. The easiest way to do this is to pick a palette (Sunlight Palette, Moonlight Palette) which you feel would look good on you and express your personality and fill most of your wardrobe these colours and shades. If you can't decide between the two, you can opt for the Universal Palette which contains shades that will look good on most people. In the upcoming chapters, I have focused on using the 'Universal palette' to accommodate for a wide range of women's colourings.

HOW TO CREATE BALANCE IN AN OUTFIT (DARK & LIGHT)

Whilst matching Sunlight colours with other Sunlight colours or Moonlight colours with other moonlight colours will always look well put together, you can take this a step further by aiming to create balance in your outfit. Balance has to be created between your **OUTFIT** (Clothing) and your **ACCESSORIES.** The easiest way to create balance is to balance dark with light (outfit vs accessories).

*Balance Dark with Light (Outfit vs Accessories)

Simply throw clothes on from your chosen palette or Universal colour scheme (as long as the shades are in the same palette), analyse your outfit (by asking yourself the question: "Does this outfit look quite light or quite dark overall?"). Then use your accessories to lighten or darken our outfit as appropriate.

As a general rule, if your outfit is dark, your accessories should be light and if your outfit is light, your accessories should be dark. The same principle applies for balancing Bright with Muted or Print with Non-Print. If your outfit is bright, your accessories should be muted and vice versa. If you have some patterns in your outfit, you should avoid having too much pattern in your accessories and vice versa.

In order to apply this to your wardrobe effectively, aim to have a wide range of colours and patterns in your tops and accessories (shoes, bags, scarves and necklaces). Even if most of your clothing colour choices are neutral colours, you will be surprised how your clothing can be transformed into something completely unique simply by changing one or two tops and/or accessories to lend colour or pattern. Remember, mixing and matching is all about the accessories!

EXAMPLES: HOW TO CREATE BALANCE IN AN OUTFIT

1.

1. SUNLIGHT PALETTE

(Sunlight with Sunlight Shades)

Creating Balance: Dark outfit/Lighter Accessories

2.

2. MOONLIGHT PALETTE

(Moonlight with Moonlight Shades)

Creating Balance: Light Outfit/Darker Accessories

3.

3. UNIVERSAL PALETTE

(Blue & Orange)

Creating Balance: Dark Outfit/ Lighter Accessories

HOW TO PUT AN OUTFIT TOGETHER

Now that you have thought about the occasion, your outfit choice in relation to the occasion, the image you want to portray and how you want to feel, you are now ready to put an outfit together. How do you go about doing this effectively? I have a simple step-by-step formula you can easily follow. I call it the BCA Formula (Base, Complement and Accentuate)

Base/Core- This is the foundation of your wardrobe and the first thing you need to create an outfit. Your base includes: Trousers, skirts, dresses and suits. Most of your base should be in neutral colours, from which you can then top up with other colour and patterns.

Complement- Your complements are what you need to wear with your base. These include: vests, tops, t-shirts, cardigans, blazers and light jackets. Your complements can be a mix of neutral and colourful shades.

Accentuate- The power of accessorising is underestimated by many. However, accessorising can make the biggest difference to maximising the use of your wardrobe and creating variety. Your Accentuates include all accessories: shoes, bags, scarves and jewellery. Your accessories should consist of a variety of colours and patterns with very few neutral colours. Ensure you have silver, gold, or other metallic jewellery on hand as these will match most of your clothing.

HOW TO CREATE A BALANCED OUTFIT USING THE BCA FORMULA (5 STEP SYSTEM)

1. Start with the **base/core of you outfit** (skirt, trousers, dress, suit) using a colour/shade in your chosen palette.

2. Then throw on something to **complement** your base (vests, tops, t-shirts, cardigans, blazers, light jackets) using another colour/shade in your chosen palette.

3. **Evaluate** your outfit so far and determine whether your outfit is '**Light**', '**Dark**' or '**Balanced**' (Top and Bottom).

4. Wear accessories to **accentuate** your outfit (shoes, bags, scarves, jewellery). Go darker with your accessories if your outfit is light and go lighter with your accessories if your outfit is dark. Go half and half if your outfit is balanced. Go bold with your accessories if your outfit is simple and keep your accessories simple if your outfit is bold.

5. Finish off your outfit with your **coat** (if required or appropriate). Your coat should preferably be a neutral colour for versatility purposes. Go light in your coat if your overall outfit is dark and dark if your overall outfit is light. In colder months, simply add a brooch to brighten up your coat if required.

Remember: There is no strict way to mix and match. Even if your outfit is not balanced in terms of 'light and dark', simply using shades in the same palette (Sunlight/ Moonlight) or Universal colour scheme will still look 'put together' even if your outfit it too dark or too light, so don't be too strict with yourself.

Use this chapter for guidance only to help you create some balance in your outfit and make getting dressed in the morning easier. When you get the hang of this method, you will find yourself taking a considerably short period of time to get dressed.

CHAPTER 6

CHAPTER 6

- YOUR CAPSULE WARDROBE -

"I want my wardrobe to be full of good clothes, so that when I'm deciding what to wear, I don't run out of options. I love shopping!"

— - Virat Kohli

Do you have trouble figuring out what to wear in the morning? Is your wardrobe overflowing with so many items of clothing that you find it hard to dig through them? Have you ever caught yourself saying "I have nothing to wear!"? If your answer is yes to all these questions, then perhaps it is time to create a good capsule wardrobe.

My definition to a 'Capsule Wardrobe' is: 'A collection of essential items of clothing and accessories that enables you to mix and match items to create a comfortable, stylish outfit for any occasion.'

From my personal experience, using a capsule wardrobe gives you a new sense of freedom. It takes away the stress of getting dressed every day, enables you to be more creative and makes you feel confident in what you are wearing. With this new found freedom, you can spend your time and brain power in other important areas of your life.

40 CAPSULE WARDROBE ESSENTIAL PIECES

The 40 essential basic pieces is a collection of essential items that you need to create a versatile wardrobe you can effortlessly mix and match, yet still look stylish and well put together. With this power list, you will always have something to wear for every occasion. You will notice that my collection of capsule wardrobe pieces does not include black. This is done intentionally to show you how you can create a range of outfit without necessarily using black.

Although I would recommend identifying with either the Sunlight palette or Moonlight palette, I have only provided illustrated examples from the Universal Palette for your capsule wardrobe pieces to accommodate most colourings. I have listed Sunlight palette and Moonlight Palette Capsule wardrobe pieces at the end of this chapter.

THE 40 CAPSULE WARDROBE ESSENTIAL PIECES - UNIVERSAL PALETTE

CLOTHING

BOTTOMS

Jeans

2 x Jeans (Plain Navy Jeans + Slightly Washed Out jeans in Navy)

Skinny or slim jeans are more versatile than any other type of jeans for the reason that you can dress them up or down with heels or flats. I also find that they look fantastic on most body shapes. Boot cut jeans are a good alternative, especially if you feel self-conscious about having larger hips.

However, boot-cut jeans don't always look great with flat shoes. Navy is a great colour for jeans because it is a great universal colour that works with ANY colour from any palette.

Plain navy jeans will always look smarter than washed out jeans, and can therefore be worn for 'smarter occasions'. Slightly washed out jeans in navy can be worn for more 'casual' occasions.

Trousers

2 x Trousers (Navy tailored Trousers + Stone Grey Chino Type Trousers)

Tailored trousers in navy will always go a long way in creating a smart outfit. A tapered leg works better for most body shapes and works with both heels and flat shoes.

Chino type trousers will provide a smarter alternative to jeans. Opting for a neutral colour in a lighter shade such as Stone Grey will enable you to create more variety in your wardrobe.

Skirts

2 x Skirts (Peach or Nude Skirt + Patterned Skirt Containing Navy or a Shade of Blue)

A peach or nude skirt will work well on most people and can be worn with many colours. Opt for a slight A-line cut for more comfort and versatility.

A patterned skirt will always look more dressed down than a block colour. Opt for your favourite pattern with at least 50% of the overall colouring being a shade of navy or blue. If you are ever stuck wondering what top to wear with your patterned skirt, always opt for a navy or soft white top.

TOPS

Sleeveless Tops

3 x Sleeveless tops (Navy, Soft White, Peach)

Sleeveless tops can change your outfit dramatically based on the colours you pick. Soft, white, plain navy and light peach colours will look great on most people and are a great starting point. Opt for smarter fabrics such as Silks, Chiffon, Wool-crepe, Polyester crepe, Lightweight tweeds, Taffeta, worsted wool, Crisp cottons and linens. These fabrics will always make your outfit look 'smarter' than a t-shirt regardless of what you wear them with. These tops can be worn under blazers, jackets or cardigans. Wearing a fitted vest under these tops will help you feel more comfortable if your chosen fabric is on the thin side!

Sleeved Tops

3 x Sleeved tops (Purple, Emerald Green, Powder Blue)

Whilst sleeveless tops will typically be worn with jackets, blazers or cardigans, sleeved tops can also be worn on their own, especially if you are not comfortable going sleeveless. Opt for more colourful pieces rather than neutral shades. I have picked purple, emerald green and powder blue, however, any accent colour in the universal palette can be used as an alternative to these colours.

V-necklines, round necklines and scoop necklines tend to work on most body shapes and necklines, including bigger busted women. If one of your problem areas is your tummy area, avoid any detail such as ruffles, folds and pleats around that area.

If your top is slightly loose, you can make it look more stylish by tucking it in loosely at the waist.

<u>Shirts</u>

1 x Shirt (Blue and White Striped Shirt)

You may be wondering why I have picked a blue and white striped shirt as opposed to the typical plain white shirt for your capsule wardrobe: Many of us own plain white shirts, but how often do we wear them? Most of us will admit to rarely wearing our white shirts. A striped white and blue shirt tends to be more versatile than a plain white one and can tend to look less formal, especially when paired with jeans.

If you are not comfortable wearing crisp textured shirts, opt for 'shirt-type' blouses in light fabrics such as silk or crepe type fabrics.

CARDIGANS AND KNITS

Cardigans

1 x Cardigan or Cape- (Medium Grey)

A medium or stone grey cardigan is a lovely neutral colour that will work with most tops and bottoms. A longer/loose cardigan will always look more stylish than a short/cropped cardigan. A cardigan will always make you look 'dressed down' and is therefore ideal for very 'casual' occasions.

<u>Sweaters</u>

1 x Sweater- (Cranberry or Burgundy)

I am personally a big fan of sweaters because they don't need much to make them look great, especially if they are colourful and have a beautiful knit on them. A deep red or burgundy colour always works a treat and looks fabulous when paired with navy jeans.

DRESSES

3 x Dresses (Plain Navy Dress, Coloured Dress (Teal), Patterned Dress Containing Blue)

A plain navy dress can easily be dressed up or down and can be used for smarter occasions. It will go with pretty much any colour or pattern you pair it with. The choice whether to go bold or simple with your overall outfit comes down to you.

Teal is a beautiful universal colour that can be worn with most sunlight colours or moonlight colours. Opt for a simple classic cut which can easily be dressed up using accessories.

A patterned dress (containing blue or navy) in your style and will prove to be a great alternative to your other dresses and will look great with most colours. Opt for a style/fabric that you can dress up or down.

JACKETS/COATS/BLAZERS

Blazers

2 x Blazers (Navy Blazer + Stone Grey Blazer)

Navy is a classic colour that will work with any colour. A navy blazer will work really well whenever you need to smarten up your outfit. Opt for a slightly textured fabric which can be worn both for professional occasions as well as smart casual occasions.

A stone grey or medium grey blazer is a light alternative to navy and will work to lighten up any dark looking outfit. Being a neutral colour, it will work well with many other colours. Opt for a textured fabric slightly different to the navy to allow for versatility.

Coats and Jackets

2 x Coats (Navy Winter Coat + Light Stone Grey Coat)

A navy coat will work with any colours you wear it with and can be thrown over dresses, skirts, trousers and even blazers. Opt for a navy winter coat with a slight fit to it or belted to give your figure some shape.

A stone Grey light coat in stone grey will work in warmer months (spring, summer and autumn) and will look particularly great with 'going out' outfits.

Casual Jacket

1 x Casual or Rain Jacket (Cranberry or Burgundy)

A padded jacket (hip or waist length) will always look stylish in a more colourful shade rather than plain black. A padded jacket will always look casual and cannot really be styled up. Therefore, colours such as blue-red, cranberry or burgundy will always add a unique, stylish twist to your casual outfit. A good alternative and more neutral shade to opt for is navy.

ACCESSORIES

Bags

1 x Main Bag Medium to Large (Navy)

We all have one of them- most likely in black. Your main bag should large enough to carry most of your stuff. A medium to large bag (depending on personal preference) would be ideal. Navy is a good choice due to its versatility. An alternative to this is dark brown.

3 x Small Shoulder bags (Powder Blue, Tan, Mustard)

Shoulder bags are often overlooked when creating a capsule wardrobe, however, they are probably one of the most important pieces in creating a diverse range of outfits. By having your shoulder bags in a variety of colours, you can add colour, style and flair to even the simplest of outfits. Powder blue, tan and mustard will provide a good range of colour options to choose from, all of which will make your outfit look unique.

1 Clutch (Nude/Light Peach)

A good quality clutch bag in a neutral colour such as nude (light peach) will work well for evening or black/white tie events. Being a neutral colour, it can be paired with any colour in the universal palette.

SHOES

Casual Shoes

1 x Ankle Boots (Dark Brown) + 1 x Loafers or Ballet Flats-
Brown

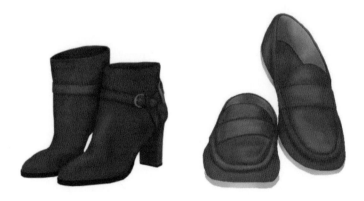

Suitable for more casual occasions, ankle boots are very
versatile and will always look fabulous with your navy jeans.
Opt for a comfortable heeled pair in dark brown colour and
a leather or suede fabric.

Brown Loafers or are great for everyday 'casual' or casual
work wear and will always look great with slim cut trousers,

skirts or dresses.

Smart Shoes

3 x Smart Shoes (Strappy/ Open Toe (Nude) + Pumps (Nude) + Colourful Patterned shoes)

Your smart shoes collection should be able to take you from day to evening whilst adding sophistication to any outfit you pair them with.

Nude strappy/open toe shoes in a block heel can be worn for day or evening, especially in warmer months.

Having a pair of comfortable pumps will be ideal for many smart occasions including work or evening.

It is important to have some other coloured shoes (plain or patterned) to add more versatility to your wardrobe. A patterned pair can add some flair to an otherwise plain or neutral outfit. Choose a pattern with colour combinations from your chosen colour palette.

SCARVES

2 x Scarves (Plain Navy Scarf + Patterned Scarf Containing Universal Shades)

Scarves can work well as accessories as well as to protect us from cold weather. Scarves tend to work particularly well when paired with blazers or coats.

A plain navy scarf will always work well on a patterned outfit containing any colour.

A colourful patterned scarf can add some flair and colour to a plain or neutral outfit.

OTHER ACCESSORIES

Necklaces

2 x Necklaces (1 chunky +1 Jewellers pendant)- A mix of silver and Gold

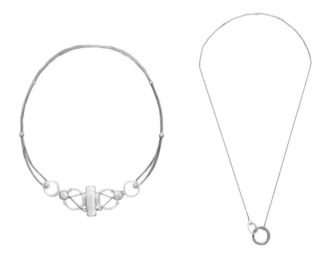

Necklaces in plain silver or gold colours will work with any outfit. I have picked a combination of silver and gold from the universal palette, however; you can easily opt for silver if your colouring is more suited to the Moonlight palette or gold if your colouring is more suited to the Sunlight palette.

A chunky necklace will improve the look of a very plain

outfit, whilst a pendant necklace will work well with any outfit you would like to 'tone-down'. Going forward, you can then introduce chunky necklaces in various colours from the Universal Platte. A pendant necklace will make any outfit look smarter.

Earrings

1 x Earrings (Studs) - (Diamante with silver or gold)

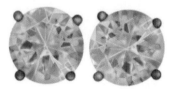

Studs are the most versatile pair of earrings you can own. They can take you from day to evening to work and always make you look smarter and well-put together.

Watches

1 x Watch (Mix of gold and silver)

I tend to prefer wearing a watch as an accessory over a bracelet. As well as being functional, a good watch will make any outfit look stylish. Watches in plain silver or gold colours will work with any outfit. I have picked a combination of silver and gold from the universal palette, however, you can easily opt for silver if your colouring is more suited to the Moonlight palette or gold if your colouring is more suited to the Sunlight palette.

Belts

1 x Waist belt (Dark Brown)

A waist belt in a dark brown colour will work with most colours and can be used to show off your waist when your outfit is loose. For those with bigger hips, it is always a good idea to also have a thin belt to wear with your jeans or trousers.

GRAND TOTAL: 40 PIECES

*For a complete list of the 40 pieces you require for the Universal Capsule Wardrobe, Sunlight Capsule Wardrobe and Moonlight Capsule Wardrobe, please visit the Appendix at the end of this book.

CHAPTER 7

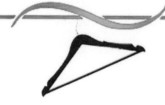

CHAPTER 7

- SMART CASUAL -

WHAT IS SMART CASUAL?

Smart casual is one of the most popular styles of this decade and a dress code that many women either do not understand or are uncertain as to how to create this look. Smart casual is essentially a neat, yet relatively informal style and can vary in degrees of 'smartness' depending on the occasion. For example, what someone might wear to go to the cinema might be more casual than what someone would wear going to dinner in a casual restaurant; yet, both outfits could be labelled as 'smart casual.'

Nailing smart casual is easy. The secret lies in balancing 'casual' clothing and accessories with 'smart' clothing and accessories.

Aim to have at least one or two pieces that are 'smart' and at least one or two pieces that are 'casual'. That is the simple secret to smart casual.

Casual fabrics include: Denim, Soft cottons & Linens, Jersey, Knits, Knitted Cottons

Smart Fabrics include: Silks, Chiffon, Wool-crepe, Polyester crepe, Lightweight tweeds, Taffeta, worsted wool, Crisp cottons and linens.

SMART CASUAL OCCASIONS

There are several ways to put together a smart casual outfit, however, I have narrowed it down to two types of occasions 'Keeping It Simple-Smart Casual' and 'Taking It Up A Notch-Smart Casual'.

EXAMPLE 1- KEEPING IT SIMPLE SMART CASUAL

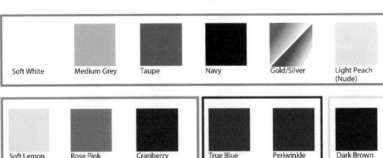

Soft White · Medium Grey · Taupe · Navy · Gold/Silver · Light Peach (Nude)

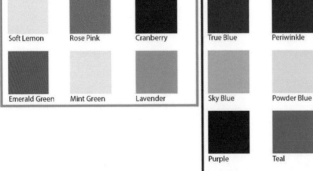

Soft Lemon · Rose Pink · Cranberry · Emerald Green · Mint Green · Lavender

True Blue · Periwinkle · Sky Blue · Powder Blue · Purple · Teal

Dark Brown · Orange · Tan · Mustard

Smart Casual- Keeping It Simple

Colour scheme: Moonlight Universal

Mixing and matching Method: Moonlight Shades with Moonlight Shades

Creating Balance method: Darker Outfit with Lighter Accessories

Types of Occasions: Going to friends for dinner, meeting friends for coffee or lunch, picking kids up from school, going to the cinema, etc.

This is the 'more casual' end of smart casual. It will typically involve wearing slightly washed out navy jeans (casual) with a smart top and a blazer or jacket. Skinny or slim jeans are more versatile than any other type of jeans for the reason that you can dress them up or down. Textured blazers will always look more casual than plain, 'office-type' blazers.

Accessories will normally be in form of ankle boots, a structured shoulder bag and a scarf. Use your bag and scarf to add a splash of colour to your outfit.

Brown boots always look classier than black for smart casual purposes and will always work with navy jeans regardless of what you wear on your top half.

EXAMPLE 2- TAKING IT UP A NOTCH SMART CASUAL

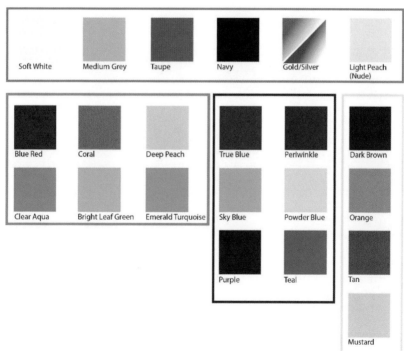

Smart Casual- Taking It Up a Notch

Colour scheme: Sunlight Universal

Mixing and Matching Method: Sunlight Shades with Sunlight Shades
Creating Balance Method: Balanced Outfit (Dark/Light) with Balanced Accessories (Dark/Light)

Types of Occasions: Dinner in a casual restaurant, meeting in-laws, day time social event, school event, day time engagement party, going to the cinema

This is the 'smarter end of smart casual. It will typically involve wearing a casual skirt (typically A-line style) or plain dark navy jeans with a smart top and smart light jacket or blazer.

Accessories can be a lot bolder. These can be added in form of a chunky necklace, colourful shoulder bag, shoes or colourful scarf.

If your outfit is dark or dull, spice it up with more colourful accessories and if your outfit is quite light or bright, you can tone down colours and patterns of your accessories typically by using neutral colours or opting for only one bold colour.

CHAPTER 8

CHAPTER 8

- EVENING WEAR -

WHAT IS EVENING WEAR?

Evening wear usually refers to 'higher-end' evening dress which includes white tie, black tie and lounge suits. I have omitted advice on style for black tie and white tie as I find the majority of women struggle more with the opposite end of evening wear- the 'less-dressed-up' end. For the purpose of this book, I would describe eveningwear as an outfit you would wear on an evening out that is a step up from smart casual. This could range from dinner out in a nice restaurant to a night out with friends.

Putting an evening wear outfit together will hugely depend on the occasion, your venue and how you want to look; however, your outfit choices should typically be 'smart' which means opting for smarter fabrics and accessories rather than casual fabrics and accessories. Smart fabrics include: Silks, Chiffon, Wool-crepe, Polyester crepe, Lightweight tweeds, Taffeta, worsted wool, Crisp cottons and Linens.

EVENING WEAR OCCASIONS

There are several ways to put together an evening outfit; however, I have narrowed it down to two types of occasions: 'Keeping It Simple-Smart Casual' and 'Taking It Up A Notch-Smart Casual'.

EXAMPLE 1- KEEPING IT SIMPLE EVENING WEAR

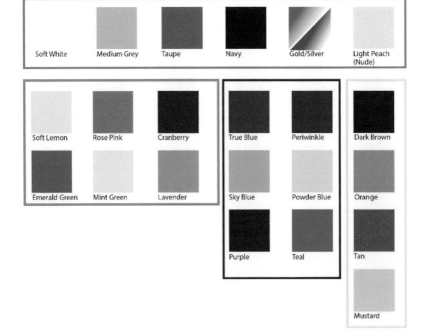

Evening Wear- Keeping It Simple

Colour scheme: Moonlight Universal

Mixing and matching Method: 'Blue and Orange'. I.e. Wear Blues with Orange, Tan or Mustard

Creating Balance method: Balanced Outfit (Light/Dark) with Balanced Accessories (Light/Dark)

Types of Occasions: Casual evening social event, dinner in a nice restaurant, night a theatre ballet or opera, first date, etc.

This is the 'less dressed-up' end of evening wear. It will typically involve wearing a less fitted or less structured patterned dress. The key is to feel extremely comfortable in your chosen style.

Accessories will normally be in the form of a simple pendant necklace, open toe shoes/sandals (with a chunky or wedge heel) or heeled ankle boots and a small structured shoulder bag.

The choice of where you add colour is entirely up to you - just remember to create balance in your overall outfit by going 'lighter' or 'darker' in your accessories depending on how 'light' or 'dark' your outfit is.

EXAMPLE 2- TAKING IT UP A NOTCH EVENING WEAR

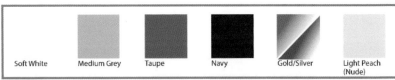

| Soft White | Medium Grey | Taupe | Navy | Gold/Silver | Light Peach (Nude) |

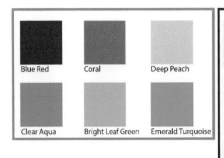

| Blue Red | Coral | Deep Peach |
| Clear Aqua | Bright Leaf Green | Emerald Turquoise |

True Blue	Periwinkle
Sky Blue	Powder Blue
Purple	Teal

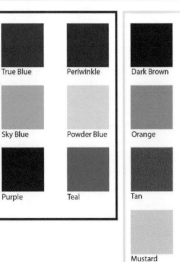

| Dark Brown |
| Orange |
| Tan |
| Mustard |

Evening Wear - Taking It Up a Notch

Colour scheme: Sunlight Universal

Mixing and matching Method: Sunlight Shades with Sunlight Shades

Creating Balance method: Balanced Outfit (Dark/Light) with Balanced Accessories (Dark/Light)

Types of Occasions: Adult birthday party, cocktail party, wedding reception, dinner at a high-end restaurant, dinner party, out for drinks, first date, etc.

This is the more 'dressed-up' end of evening wear. It will typically involve wearing a more fitted or more structured dress. You will always feel very dressed up in this outfit, although there are occasions where you may want to be particularly dressed up.

Accessories will normally be in the form of a simple pendant necklace or a chunkier extravagant piece depending on your choice of outfit. Shoes could be closed or open as in the case of sandals, with a pointed heel. A clutch bag may be used in this case.

The choice of where you add colour is entirely up to you and how you want to feel- just remember to create balance in your overall outfit.

CHAPTER 9

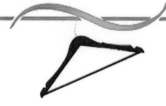

CHAPTER 9

- PROFESSIONAL WORK-WEAR -

WHAT IS PROFESSIONAL WORK-WEAR?

For the purpose of this book, I will describe professional work wear as an outfit you would wear to work. Putting an outfit together in this category will hugely depend on your workplace culture, the type of industry you work in and how much freedom you have in your outfit choices. I cannot cater for every industry; however, I hope the ideas in this chapter provide some inspiration for your type of workplace.

Your outfit choices should be typically 'smart' which means opting for smarter fabrics and accessories rather than casual fabrics and accessories such as jeans and t-shirts, especially if you are in a client front-facing industry. Structured clothing will make you look smarter and more professional. Smart fabrics include: Silks, Chiffon, Wool-crepe, Polyester crepe, Lightweight tweeds, Taffeta, worsted wool, Crisp cottons and Linens.

PROFESSIONAL WORK-WEAR OCCASIONS

There are several ways to put together an evening outfit; however, I have narrowed it down to two types of occasions: 'Keeping it simple- Professional work wear and 'taking it up a notch- Professional work wear.

EXAMPLE 1- KEEPING IT SIMPLE PROFESSIONAL WORK WEAR

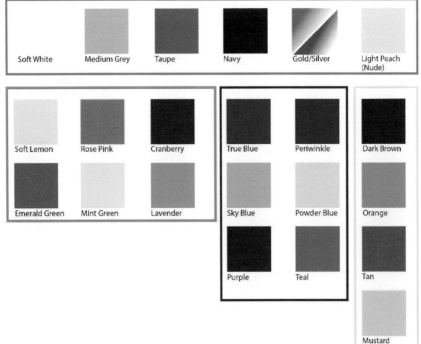

| Soft White | Medium Grey | Taupe | Navy | Gold/Silver | Light Peach (Nude) |

| Soft Lemon | Rose Pink | Cranberry |
| Emerald Green | Mint Green | Lavender |

True Blue	Periwinkle
Sky Blue	Powder Blue
Purple	Teal

| Dark Brown |
| Orange |
| Tan |
| Mustard |

Professional Work Wear- Keeping It Simple

Colour scheme: Moonlight Universal

Mixing and matching Method: Moonlight Shades with Moonlight Shades

Creating Balance method: Darker Outfit with Lighter Accessories

Types of Occasions: Informal daily work wear, casual Fridays, creative industries, working from home (and may need to go out), informal job interviews, etc.

This is the less 'dressed-up' end of professional work wear. It will typically involve wearing neutral coloured tailored trousers (preferably with some stretch), a smart top with or without a blazer and flat shoes or shoes with a very small/ chunky heel. If wearing a blazer; opt for a more textured type such as tweed, rather than a plain 'office style' blazer. They key is to look professional, yet comfortable in this style.

Accessories will normally be in form of a simple pendant necklace, a structured bag and flat closed shoes or shoes with a very small/ chunky heel.

The choice of where you add colour depends on your workplace culture or how you want to look that day. Some workplaces are restricted to more neutral tones, in which case you could only add a pop of colour using your top or accessories. More creative industries can opt for more colour; in which case, you could add more colour in your clothing choices.

EXAMPLE 2- TAKING IT UP A NOTCH PROFESSIONAL WORK WEAR

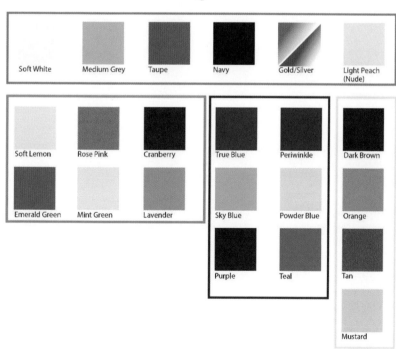

Soft White	Medium Grey	Taupe	Navy	Gold/Silver	Light Peach (Nude)

Soft Lemon	Rose Pink	Cranberry
Emerald Green	Mint Green	Lavender

True Blue	Periwinkle
Sky Blue	Powder Blue
Purple	Teal

Dark Brown
Orange
Tan
Mustard

Professional Work Wear - Taking It Up a Notch

Colour scheme: Sunlight Universal

Mixing and matching Method: Sunlight Shades with Sunlight Shades

Creating Balance method: Balanced Outfit (Dark/Light) with Balanced Accessories (Dark/Light)

Types of Occasions: Corporate office, management role, business lunch, office party, doing presentations, etc.

This is the 'more dressed-up' end of professional work wear. It will typically involve wearing a structured suit or fitted/structured dress.

Accessories will normally be in form of a simple pendant necklace or a stylish brooch, depending on your choice of outfit. Shoes could be closed, pointed and have some form of heel. Your choice of bag should be structured. Scarves should be in a soft 'silk-like' fabric as this will always make your outfit look smarter and more professional.

Colour can be added in small amounts through tops, scarves or brooches. For those in industries where you have more freedom to add colour, you could do so in form of a dress or jacket. Again, remember to create balance in your overall outfit by going 'lighter' or 'darker' in your accessories depending on how 'light' or 'dark' your outfit is.

CHAPTER 10

CHAPTER 10

- WARDROBE REVIEW AND WEEDING -

*"Get rid of clutter and you may just find
that it was blocking the door you've been
looking for."*

— *Katrina Mayer*

C reating a mix and match wardrobe doesn't stop at having the knowledge to create a varied range of outfits. Having the knowledge to create a great mix and match wardrobe is one thing, but putting it into practice can be a challenge. Sorting through your wardrobe and banishing wardrobe clutter is a good place to start. By performing a lifestyle review, a wardrobe review and a wardrobe weeding session, you will be in the perfect position to build a stylish and functional mix and match wardrobe that is suited to you and your lifestyle.

DO YOU HAVE A TOXIC WARDROBE?

Most women are guilty of having what I refer to as a 'toxic wardrobe'. A toxic wardrobe is a cluttered wardrobe. It is a wardrobe full of clothing, shoes and accessories that are under-used and are unworkable.

You have a toxic wardrobe if:

- You have clothing in your wardrobe you have not worn for the last 2 years
- Your clothes are very closely packed together you

barely have space to add any more.

- You have clothing in your wardrobe that is not functional (too big, too small, wrong styles, wrong colours, clothing you simply don't love or clothing and accessories not related to your current lifestyle).

- You have clothing in your wardrobe that reminds you of a sad time in your life, such as a break up or job loss.

For various reasons, such as shopping without purpose, blindly following fashion trends, copy-cat dressing or lack of knowledge about what works for you, you may have ended up accumulating an excessive, non-workable wardrobe-Having clothing and accessories in your wardrobe that you don't use. The solution to this is an initial wardrobe review based on your current lifestyle as well as a wardrobe weeding session.

LIFESTYLE REVIEW

Most women have plenty of clothes in their wardrobes, yet still struggle to get dressed in the morning. This is partly caused by failing to take into consideration your lifestyle when building your wardrobe. Ideally, your wardrobe should be proportional to your lifestyle. Pie charts are a good way of determining the required focus for your wardrobe and separating your clothes into work/weekend/social wardrobes. Let's treat your week as 100% (or if you struggle with percentages, treat your full week as a 10). Now, assign percentages to the amount of time you spend at the following:

Work: This could be office, meeting clients, working from home, etc.

Informal Socialising: Afternoon meet-ups, networking events, casual restaurants, bars/pubs, theatre, etc.

Night Out: Night out with friends, bars, dinner, parties, events, etc.

Home and Everyday Stuff: Home, food shopping, running kids to and from school, etc.

Other: If there is something else that you spend a considerable amount of time on that can't be allocated to any of the above sections, add it to 'Other'. An example of this would include: Exercising (gym, Swimming, Walking, etc.).

Simply split your average week up into your different activities.

Next, draw a large circle and apportion your week (in relation to time spent doing these activities) to various 'slices' of the pie. The larger the slice, the more time you spend doing that activity. A simpler way to do this is creating a pie chart on a word document. From this pie chart, you will be able to tailor your wardrobe more efficiently. You can, for example, ensure you do not have multiple 'night out' dresses when, in fact, this only amounts to 10% of your week.

EXAMPLE: LIFESTYLE ACTIVITY DIVIDE

My lifestyle activity divide and pie chart will look like this:

LIFESTYLE ACTIVITY	LIFESTYLE ACTIVITY DIVIDE		
Work	3.5	35%	
Informal Socialising	1.5	15%	
Night Out	1	10%	
Home and Everyday Stuff	2.5	25%	
Other (Gym & Exercise)	1.5	15%	
TOTAL	**10**	**100%**	

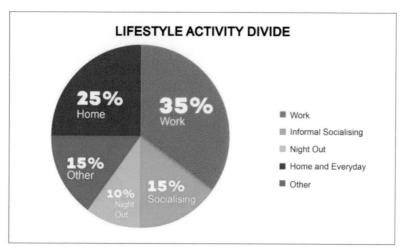

From the table and pie chart above, you can clearly see that I spend most of my time at work (35%) and at home (25%), which means that the majority of my wardrobe should be clothing and accessories that I can wear for these elements of my lifestyle.

WARDROBE REVIEW

Next, look into your wardrobe and evaluate if your wardrobe reflects your current lifestyle. Think about what kind of outfits you need in each category and create your wardrobe accordingly. For example, my work mainly involves meeting clients on an informal basis and therefore most of my work wardrobe is based on 'Smart casual' attire. For this reason, most of my wardrobe is composed of jeans, smart tops, blazers and plenty of accessories to be able to create a range of outfits from a variety of individual pieces. You may find that some categories overlap, for example. As a stylist, I will tend to wear similar clothing for 'work' and 'informal socialising', therefore; my wardrobe contains clothing and accessories that reflect this divide (i.e. 'Smart Casual'). The whole point of this exercise is to ensure you have enough clothing and accessories to create a range of outfits for any occasion.

HOW TO PERFORM A WARDROBE WEEDING SESSION:

Now that you have reviewed your lifestyle, it is time to create and build your ideal wardrobe. Performing a wardrobe weeding session is not an easy process. Most of us love to hold on to things, even if we know deep down that these things are no longer working for us. The success of this process relies on you being completely honest with yourself and mentally preparing yourself to let go of the old and welcome the new.

Remember that whatever you keep that is not working for you is taking away your energy (physically, mentally and emotionally) and of course the perfect opportunity to create your ideal mix and match wardrobe. Imagine a wardrobe where each and every item of clothing and accessory is usable? Imagine a wardrobe full of clothing and accessories that you can mix and match, easily throw on and look stylish every single time? In order to get yourself to this place, you will need to create the space and energy for the 'new' to come in. Holding on to the 'old' stifles any progress. For this reason, you will have to be extremely strict with yourself throughout this process. Trust me; it will all be worth it in the end!

You can perform a wardrobe weeding session 4 times a year (after every season) or twice a year. I tend to perform a wardrobe weeding session twice a year; just before Spring (for Spring and Summer) and just before Autumn (for Autumn and Winter).

Here is a step by step process on how to perform a wardrobe weeding session:

Step 1

Plan in a day or two in your diary where you can carry out a wardrobe weeding session- undisturbed. Divide your wardrobe weeding themes into three, namely: 'All clothes that you wear out', 'Clothing that you wear in the house or for exercise' and 'Shoes and other accessories'. In order to avoid getting too overwhelmed with the whole process, pick one theme per session or day.

Step 2

Pick a colour palette based on what you feel resonates with you the most and use this palette as your basis for your choice of colours for the clothing and accessories in your wardrobe. If you have picked more than one palette, separate your wardrobe arrangement to clearly separate the two palettes. Remember, colour makes the biggest difference when it comes to mixing and matching.

Step 3

Find 3 pieces of A4 paper and 4 stick labels. Create 3 main piles and label them: 'Love, 'Ok' and 'Wrong' piles. Then find 4 big and strong bin bags or boxes ad label them: 'Not in season', 'Resale', 'Charity' and 'Bin'.

Go through your whole wardrobe, analysing each piece of clothing or accessory you have and placing each piece on the 'Love', 'Ok' or 'Wrong' piles.

'Love Pile': This consists of items that you absolutely love.

They should match your chosen palette of colours and the style/cut should sit well on your body. You should be able to feel 100% comfortable in these pieces.

'OK Pile': This consists of items you like, but don't love. It should also consist of items you do not wear frequently or those you are not sure about.

'Wrong Pile': This consists of pieces that you have not worn in the last two years for different reasons. It could be that you dislike them, they are either too small or too big, they are the wrong styles or colours for you or you just do not see yourself wearing them again.

Step 4

From the 3 piles, do the following:

Love Pile: Remove items that are not in season and put these in the 'Not in season' box or suitcase. I personally tend to have 'Spring' and 'Summer' Pieces together and 'Autumn' and 'Winter' pieces together. The remainder of your clothing should go back into your wardrobe. Ensure you hand as many pieces as possible that you would wear out to make the most of them. Always perform another review of the clothing you put away before you return them to your wardrobe to ensure they still work for your taste and lifestyle.

OK Pile: Analyse each piece and keep the pieces you think you will definitely wear in that particular season. Put the rest in the 'Not in season' box or suitcase to be analysed again when you perform your next wardrobe declutter, most likely at the start of a new season. If at your next weeding session you have missed these pieces, put them back in your wardrobe. If you feel you have not missed them and can do without them, add them to the 'Resale' or 'Charity' pile.

Wrong Pile: Analyse each piece and organise accordingly according to the following:

'Resale'- This bag or box is for good quality items you would like to resale and you are absolutely sure you will have the time to sell them either through websites such as eBay or clothing exchange shops. Otherwise, give these away to

family and friends.

'Charity'- Have a bin bag where you can put all clothing and accessories in this pile and be sure to take it to the charity shop the same day!

'Bin'- this is for badly worn items that cannot be sold or taken to charity. Put them in a bin bag right away and get rid of them the same day.

*Remember, you should only be left with clothing and accessories that you love in colours and styles that complement you. Whatever is left in your wardrobe should be suitable for your lifestyle.

Step 4

Whatever clothing and accessories are left should go back into your wardrobe and arranged in such a way that you can see most of your clothing and get as much wear out of them as possible. Hang as many clothes as possible in your wardrobe rather than fold them and invest in good quality hangers that will help prolong the life of your clothing. The only clothing that should be folded should be your workout clothing, very casual t-shirts, underwear and scarves. Have these in separate drawers.

The best way to arrange your clothing and accessories in your wardrobe is according to categories and colours (shades). All tops, dresses, skirts, trousers, jackets & blazers as well as coats should be hung in their respective sections according to their different colours and shades. Also, have lighter shades together, darker shades together and patterned shades together. It is also a good idea to separate your pieces according to fabric. Smarter fabrics should be separated from casual fabrics.

Your bags and necklaces should always be on display for you to get the most wear out of them. Ensure you have your earrings and brooches in a jewellery box that is easily accessible. You will also use your shoulder bags more if they are hang up and easily accessible. Remember, getting dressed for any occasion is only as easy as how organised and accessible your wardrobe is.

CHAPTER 11

CHAPTER 11

- HOW TO BECOME A SMART SHOPPER -

"Fashion is about dressing according to what's fashionable. Style is more about being yourself."

— Oscar de la Renta

Now that you have created space in your wardrobe, it is time to fill the gaps in your wardrobe by acquiring clothing or accessories you need. It is time for a shopping trip! The important thing to remember is you do not have to do this all at once, especially if you don't have the luxury of spending lots of money on a new wardrobe. You can do this over a period of 6 months, one, two or even three years. The most important thing is that you LOVE what you buy and that it works for your wardrobe and lifestyle. Be patient and opt for quality over quantity. Eventually, you will get there!

Here are some tips on how to become a smart shopper and make the most of your shopping trips:

Forget Fashion Trends

I completely understand why certain people follow fashion trends religiously. We are drawn to the new and novel. In my opinion, fashion trends should only be looked at as a source of inspiration from which we can draw our own ideas about style. We should be able to draw on our own personal style to pick out what is relevant to us out of the available fashion choices. If we make the decision to buy only what flatters us and works with our lifestyle, we are not allowing fashion to dictate our wardrobes-and consequently our lives. We are empowering ourselves to be in control of what we wear and how we wear it. This is the definition of real style.

Shop Less Frequently

How frequently do you shop? Weekly? Monthly? Seasonally? According to past experience, shopping too frequently for clothing is very likely to contribute to having a cluttered wardrobe. It causes us to be less creative with and wear less of what we already have; opting to wear only what is new. Shopping frequently also results in more spending and in some extreme cases, unwanted debt. Shopping less frequently will allow you to be more creative with what you already have and save lots of money in the long run.

How frequently should you shop? This is a choice that has to be made on an individual basis. I personally prefer to have two big shopping trips twice a year prioritising the most important pieces in my wardrobe (core pieces I wear the most) such as jeans, blazers, ankle boots and a few tops. The rest of the year, I will top up with only a few pieces if and when I need them or when I see something I absolutely love and want to treat myself to.

Save Monthly for Shopping

Do you sometimes feel guilty for buying something that you feel you do not necessarily need? Do you sometimes find yourself feeling you don't have enough money to buy what you want or need? Having some savings purely for shopping purposes will make you feel less guilty about your clothing purchases, enjoy shopping a lot more and enable you to make the most of your money. For example, saving £100 monthly provides you with £600 for your big bi-annual shopping trips which means you are more likely to buy better quality clothing and potentially get a lot more clothing for your money depending on where and when you shop.

Write a Shopping List

Planning is key to getting the best of your wardrobe or shopping sessions. After having performed a wardrobe weeding session, refer to your capsule wardrobe list and look for anomalies. Ensure you prioritise 'needs' over wants according to your lifestyle. For example, most of my lifestyle involves me wearing 'smart casual'. For this reason, I will opt for jeans and other casual trousers in favour of tailored trousers. In comparison, someone working full time in a corporate environment would perhaps opt for tailored trousers, skirts and dresses.

Write a shopping list before you go out shopping based on gaps in your wardrobe. Ensure you have a budget and be clear about how much you want to spend. Be very strict with your purchases opting for quality over quantity and try to stick to your budget as much as possible.

Plan Which Shops to Visit or Buy From (Online)

Planning which shops to visit saves time and money on wasted purchases. Your shopping trip will be a lot more focussed and you are more likely to have a successful shopping trip. Look at your shopping list and think of shops you are likely to acquire these pieces for the best possible quality at the best possible prices. One thing to be aware of is that no shop does all types of clothing extremely well. From past experience, you cannot acquire a good capsule wardrobe from only one type of brand or shop.

If there are shops you love for specific types of clothing, sticking to what you know doesn't hurt, unless you have been recommended a different brand that you think might work well for your body shape; in which case, it is a good idea to try something new. For example, if you are someone that struggles to get a good pair of jeans that works for you but you have found a brand or shop whose jeans you absolutely love on you, try that brand first for options before trying other shops.

Opt for Quality over Quantity

Before becoming a stylist, I was of the mind-set that buying more clothes, even if there were of poor quality would be better because you have more clothing to create outfits with. Experience has proved me completely wrong! A wardrobe full of quality clothing and accessories is much more versatile, practical and long-lasting. The benefits of having a wardrobe with quality pieces are endless; you will save more money long term, love your wardrobe more and look well put together. Your clothing will always feel better on and you will be much more confident in how you mix and match your clothing and accessories knowing that each individual piece looks and feels great on you.

Focus, Focus, Focus - How Not to Get Overwhelmed When Shopping

When out shopping, some women feel completely overwhelmed by the presence of hundreds of items of clothing and accessories in different styles and colours, whilst others feel intimidated by other shoppers or hate being approached by Sales Assistants. There are many ways to overcome this and have a more enjoyable shopping trip or online shopping experience. The easiest way to do this is by consciously being in your 'own zone'. This means 'zoning-out' other people and instead focusing on yourself and your needs.

Once you walk into a shop, walk straight to the section where you will find what you need. For example, if you have '5 tops' on your shopping list, go to the sections where you will find tops. To start with, look out for colours in our chosen palette, then analyse these, opting to try on only styles and patterns that you love and ones you feel will work best on your body shape. This process will save you plenty of time and be less overwhelming than looking at each and every garment in the shop as an option.

AFTER SHOPPING

After your shopping trip, leave your purchased clothing and accessories in your bags or hand them up with tags still on. Try them on the next day and check to see if you love them and will definitely wear them. If in any doubt, return them. If you are happy with your purchases, remove the tags and hang them up in the relevant categories of your wardrobe.

FINAL WORDS

We have reached the end of the No Black Project. I hope that the information in this book has inspired you to take more control of your wardrobe and experiment with different outfit combinations. My hope is that this book transforms your personal style and wardrobe and gives you the confidence to become more creative in how you build your wardrobe and consequently, your outfits for various occasions.

While there is no set 'code' or 'rules' when it comes to personal style, having some guidelines can guide us in our fashion and style choices, helping us to enjoy fashion and style, save time and energy and save money long term. These guidelines will essentially make the most of our wardrobes. As you begin working with the suggested colour palettes and capsule wardrobe pieces, you will learn that there is no limit to the possible outfit combinations you can create. Remember that the capsule wardrobe pieces are just the foundation or skeleton of your wardrobe. Use the information in this book as a basis from which you can add your own stamp and make it work for you and your lifestyle. Always remember that whilst you can have as many black pieces as you want, you do not NEED black, there are so many fun outfits you can create without it that will ensure your wardrobe is more versatile. My personal wardrobe is proof of that.

Take every occasion (small or big) as a perfect opportunity to unleash your creativity and experiment with different outfit combinations. Soon, you will realise that you do not have to have thousands of items of clothing and accessories in your wardrobe to look fabulous every day.

SHARE AND REVIEW

I wrote this book from the heart: To share things I have learnt over the years that have been transformative for me. To be honest, I was a little scared to do it, putting myself out there and exposing myself to the world. But friends and clients who have applied the principles pushed me into writing it. Being pregnant with my first son Spencer also motivated me to complete this book. If it wasn't for the immense support from friends, family and clients, this book would not exist.

That is the beauty of learning, and then sharing. You grow, and you help other people grow. You improve your life and encourage others to do the same. I hope you try out what I have shared in this book and learn a thing or two from it that you can apply to your life.

Working on this book took a lot of commitment and hard work. My sincere hope is that it reaches as many women as possible all over the world. For this reason, your review is really important to me. Please take some time to review this book on *Amazon* or share with friends on *social media*. Thank you.

ABOUT THE AUTHOR

I am fortunate enough to have had some amazing experiences in my life so far, but the most transformative experience has been the simple act of loving my body and learning to simplify my own wardrobe - and consequently, my lifestyle. One of the best decisions I have ever made in my life was to become a Personal Stylist and help hundreds of women improve their personal style and become more confident. My passion is teaching women the skills to look their best and create wardrobes that are both flattering and in line with their lifestyles. I have written this book to help women appreciate their bodies, simplify their wardrobes and create effortless mix and match wardrobes.

You can find me online here:

- The No Black Project Book Information and Blog: www.thenoblackproject.com
- Personal Styling Website: www.stylemeflawless.co.uk

- Personal Website

  www.numba-pinkerton.co.uk

The No Black Project Challenge

The No Black Project Challenge is a minimalist mix and match fashion challenge that invites you to avoid wearing black for a month.

By training yourself not to heavily rely on black, you open yourself up to the possibility of creating a better mix and match wardrobe, so that you always have a stylish outfit for every occasion. You will also be contributing towards fashion sustainability by using more of the pieces you currently own.

Join women from around the world who have accepted the challenge and are now living fuller lives.

For details on how to take part in The No Black Project Challenge, visit www.thenoblackproject.com

Please feel free to email me at stylemeflawless@live.com

I would be honoured if you reviewed this book on *Amazon*.

Thank you.

CREDITS 1

RACHAEL HOOD - ILLUSTRATOR

It is my pleasure to introduce the person behind my lovely illustrations of the 'Capsule Wardrobe 40 Pieces' and '9 Outfits' used in this book- Rachael Hood.

Rachael Hood works as a Freelance Illustrator and Film-maker. She is originally from Edinburgh and is now based in Glasgow, Scotland. Rachael studied Communication Design at Glasgow School of Art (GSA) and also spent a semester at Emily Carr University of Art and Design, Vancouver.

Rachael's approach to image making has continually evolved, allowing her to develop a broad skills base and giving her the flexibility to apply those skills to a variety of projects where applicable. Rachael's illustration work specialises in print-making, enjoying the craftsmanship and handmade quality that these methods can provide.

As a young practitioner, Rachael has already achieved a considerable resume. She has been involved in a diverse range of non-profit, humanitarian projects including running a skills based art course in a prison, mural painting for the children's charity- 'Barnardos' and co-founding a food waste reduction and meal sharing community operating out of GSA. This collaborative work has continued into the field of design, with Rachael working within the Branding and

Identity Team for the BBC Arts Online live stage production of 'Dream On'. Other projects include working on a short film as writer, director and cinematographer and writing an adult narrative book, containing individually hand-printed illustrations.

Please visit: www.rachael-hood.com

CREDITS 2

I would like to express my sincere gratitude to the following people for their patience and perseverance in the production of this book:

- Capsule Wardrobe 40 Pieces and 9 Outfits Illustrations- Rachael Hood
- Colour Palettes & Charts Illustrations- Anca Loana Bostina
- Book Editor- Laura Wilkinson
- Cover Designer- PixelStudio
- Book Production- BookClaw

APPENDIX 1

LIST OF 40 CAPSULE WARDROBE ESSENTIAL PIECES (UNIVERSAL PALETTE)

CLOTHING

BOTTOMS

- 2 x Jeans (Plain Navy + Navy Slightly Washed)
- 1 x Tailored Trousers (Navy)
- 1 x Chino Type Trousers (Stone Grey)
- 2 x Skirts (Peach + Patterned Containing Navy or Blue)

Total 6

TOPS

- 3 x Sleeveless tops (Navy, White, Peach)
- 3 x Blouses/sleeved tops (Purple, Emerald Green, Powder Blue)
- 1 x Shirt (Blue and White Striped Shirt)

Total 7

CARDIGANS AND KNITS

- 1 x Cardigan or Cape- (Medium Grey)
- 1 x Sweater- (Cranberry or Burgundy)

Total 2

DRESSES

- 1 x Universal Dress- (Navy) DRESSES
- 1 x Coloured Dress- (Teal or Purple)
- 1 x Patterned Dress- (Containing Navy or Blue)

Total 3

JACKETS/COATS/BLAZERS

- 2 x Blazers (Navy + Stone)
- 1 x Winter Coat (Navy)
- 1 x Light Coat (Stone)
- 1 x Casual or Rain Jacket (Blue-red, Raspberry or Burgundy)

Total 5

ACCESSORIES

BAGS

- 1 x Main Bag Medium to Large (Navy)
- 3 x Small Shoulder Bags (Tan, Mustard, Powder Blue)
- 1 Clutch (Nude/Light Peach)

Total 5

SHOES

- 1 x Ankle Boots (Dark Brown)
- 1 x Loafers or Ballet Flats- Brown
- 1 x Strappy/ Open Toe (Brown or Nude)
- 1 x Pumps (Nude)
- 1 x Colourful Patterned Shoes- (Any colour combination from the Universal palette)

Total 5

SCARVES

- 1 x Plain Scarf (Navy)
- 1 x Patterned Scarf (Any colour combination from the Universal palette)

Total 2

OTHER ACCESSORIES

- 2 x Necklaces (1 chunky, 1 Jewellers pendant)- A mix of silver and Gold
- 1 x Earrings (Studs)- (Diamante with silver or gold)
- 1 x Watch (mix of gold and silver)
- 1 x Waist belt (Dark Brown)

Total 5

GRAND TOTAL: 40

40 CAPSULE WARDROBE ESSENTIAL PIECES (SUNLIGHT PALETTE)

CLOTHING

BOTTOMS

- 2 x Jeans (Plain + Navy Slightly washed)
- 1 x Tailored Trousers (Navy)
- 1 x Chino Type Trousers (Beige)
- 2 x Skirts (Peach/Nude + Patterned Containing Navy or Blue)

Total 6

TOPS

- 3 x Sleeveless tops (Cream, Peach, Navy)
- 3 x Blouses/sleeved tops (Coral, Mustard, Periwinkle Blue)
- 1 x Shirt (Blue and White lined shirt)

Total 7

CARDIGANS AND KNITS

- 1 x Cardigan- (Beige)
- 1 x Sweater- (Khaki, Rust or Bittersweet Red)

Total 2

DRESSES

- 1 x Universal Dress- (Navy)
- 1 x Colourful Dress (Sunlight shade of your choice- Options include: Salmon, Teal, Purple or Orange)
- 1 x Patterned Dress (Any Sunlight shades of your choice or a pattern containing Navy)

Total 3

JACKETS/COATS/BLAZERS

- 2 x Blazers (Navy and Carmel)
- 1 x Light Coat (beige)
- 1 x Structured Winter Coat (Navy)
- 1 x Padded Casual/Rain Jacket (Bittersweet Red, Khaki or Navy)

Total 5

ACCESSORIES

BAGS

- 1 x Main Bag Medium to Large (Dark Brown or Tan)
- 3 x Small Shoulder bags (Tan, Mustard, Tomato Red)
- 1 Clutch (Nude/Light Peach)

Total 5

SHOES

- 1 x Ankle Boots (Dark Brown)
- 1 x Loafers or Ballet Flats- Brown
- 1 x Strappy/ Open Toe (Brown or Nude)
- 1 x Pumps (Nude)
- 1 x Colourful Patterned shoes- (Any colour combination from the Sunlight palette)

Total 5

SCARVES

- 1 x Plain Scarf (Navy)
- 1 x Patterned Scarf (Any colour combination from the Sunlight palette)

Total 2

OTHER ACCESSORIES

- 2 x Necklaces (1 chunky, 1 Jewellers pendant)- Gold (Including Rose Gold)
- 1 x Earrings (Studs)- (Diamante with gold)
- 1 x Watch (Gold)
- 1 x Waist belt (Dark Brown)

Total 5

GRAND TOTAL: 40

40 CAPSULE WARDROBE ESSENTIAL PIECES-MOONLIGHT PALETTE

<u>CLOTHING</u>

BOTTOMS

- 2 x Jeans (Plain + Navy Slightly washed)
- 1 x Tailored Trousers (Navy)
- 1 x Chino Type Trousers (Medium Grey)
- 2 x Skirts (Burgundy + Patterned Containing Navy or Blue)

Total 6

TOPS

- 3 x Sleeveless tops (White, Powder Blue, Navy)
- 3 x Blouses/sleeved tops (Magenta or Fuchsia, Mint Green, Blue-Red)
- 1 x Shirt (Blue and White lined shirt)

Total 7

CARDIGANS AND KNITS

- 1 x Cardigan- (Medium or Light Grey)
- 1 x Sweater- (Burgundy or Cranberry)

Total 2

DRESSES

- 1 x Universal Dress- (Navy)
- 1 x Colourful Dress (Moonlight shade of your choice- Options include: True Green, Teal, Cobalt Blue or Burgundy)
- 1 x Patterned Dress (Any Moonlight shades of your choice or a pattern containing Navy)

Total 3

JACKETS/COATS/BLAZERS

- 2 x Blazers (Navy and Medium Grey)
- 1 x Light Coat (Stone Grey)
- 1 x Structured Winter Coat (Navy)
- 1 x Padded Casual/Rain Jacket (Cranberry Red, Burgundy or Navy)

Total 5

ACCESSORIES

BAGS

- 1 x Main Bag Medium to Large (Navy or Deep Brown)
- 3 x Small Shoulder bags (Powder Blue, Magenta, True Green)
- 1 Clutch (Silver/Light grey)

Total 5

SHOES

- 1 x Ankle Boots (Deep Brown)
- 1 x Loafers or Ballet Flats- Deep Brown
- 1 x Strappy/ Open Toe (Navy or Deep Brown)
- 1 x Pumps (Navy)
- 1 x Colourful Patterned shoes- (Any colour combination from the Moonlight palette)

Total 5

SCARVES

- 1 x Plain Scarf (Navy)
- 1 x Patterned Scarf (Any colour combination from the Moonlight palette)

Total 2

OTHER ACCESSORIES

- 2 x Necklaces (1 chunky, 1 Jewellers pendant)- Silver
- 1 x Earrings (Studs)- (Diamante with silver)
- 1 x Watch (Silver)
- 1 x Waist belt (Deep Brown)

Total 5

GRAND TOTAL: 40

APPENDIX 2

COLOUR PALETTES

UNIVERSAL SHADES

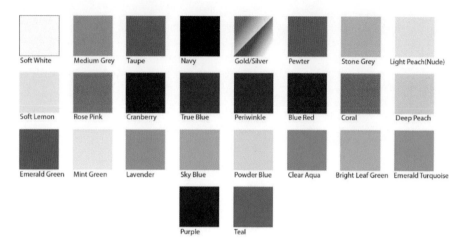

MOONLIGHT SHADES

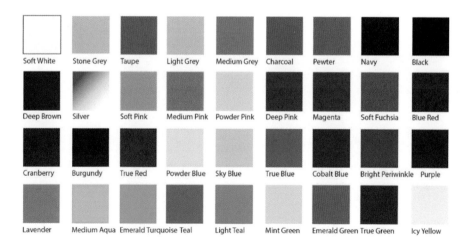

SUNLIGHT SHADES

Ivory	Cream	Stone Grey	Taupe	Beige	Carmel	Tan	Dark Brown	Orange

Burnt Orange	Mustard	Warm Yellow	Light Peach	Deep Peach	Salmon	Coral	Mango	Tomato Red

Bittersweet Red	Rust	Deep Khaki	Khaki	Lime Green	Pastel Yellow Green	Forest Green	Olive	Teal

Turquoise	Emerald Turquoise	Navy	Periwinkle	Hyacinth Blue	Aqua	Purple	Warm Violet	Gold

18781307R00119

Printed in
by Ama
Poland